Mindset Mathematics

Visualizing and Investigating Big Ideas

Jo Boaler

Jen Munson

Cathy Williams

JB JOSSEY-BASS™

A Wiley Brand

Published by Jossey-Bass
A Wiley Brand
One Montgomery Street, Suite 1000, San Francisco, CA 94104-4594—www.josseybass.com

Jossey-Bass books and products are available through most bookstores. To contact Jossey-Bass directly call our Customer Care Department within the U.S. at 800-956-7739, outside the U.S. at 317-572-3986, or fax 317-572-4002.

Wiley publishes in a variety of print and electronic formats and by print-on-demand. Some material included with standard print versions of this book may not be included in e-books or in print-on-demand. If this book refers to media such as a CD or DVD that is not included in the version you purchased, you may download this material at http://booksupport.wiley.com. For more information about Wiley products, visit www.wiley.co

Library of Congress Cataloging-in-Publication Data are available

ISBN 978-1-119-35871-8 (paper); ISBN 978-1-119-35878-7 (ebk.); ISBN 978-1-11935876-3 (ebk.)

Cover design by Wiley
Cover image: © Marish/Shutterstock-Eye; © Kritchanut/iStockphoto-Background
Printed in the United States of America

FIRST EDITION

PB Printing   10 9 8 7 6 5 4 3 2 1

Contents

To all those teachers pursuing a mathematical mindset journey with us.

Introduction

I still remember the moment when Youcubed, the Stanford center I direct, was conceived. I was at the Denver NCSM and NCTM conferences in 2013, and I had arranged to meet Cathy Williams, the director of mathematics for Vista Unified School District. Cathy and I had been working together for the past year improving mathematics teaching in her district. We had witnessed amazing changes taking place, and a filmmaker had documented some of the work. I had recently released my online teacher course, called How to Learn Math, and been overwhelmed by requests from tens of thousands of teachers to provide them with more of the same ideas. Cathy and I decided to create a website and use it to continue sharing the ideas we had used in her district and that I had shared in my online class. Soon after we started sharing ideas on the Youcubed website, we were invited to become a Stanford University center, and Cathy became the codirector of the center with me.

In the months that followed, with the help of one of my undergraduates, Montse Cordero, our first version of youcubed.org was launched. By January 2015, we had managed to raise some money and hire engineers, and we launched a revised version of the site that is close to the site you may know today. We were very excited that in the first month of that relaunch, we had five thousand visits to the site. At the time of writing this, we are now getting three million visits to the site each month. Teachers are excited to learn about the new research and to take the tools, videos, and activities that translate research ideas into practice and use them in their teaching.

Low-Floor, High-Ceiling Tasks

One of the most popular articles on our website is called "Fluency without Fear." I wrote this with Cathy when I heard from many teachers that they were being made to use timed tests in the elementary grades. At the same time, new brain science was emerging showing that when people feel stressed—as students do when facing a timed test—part of their brain, the working memory, is restricted. The working memory is exactly the area of the brain that comes into play when students need to calculate with math facts, and this is the exact area that is impeded when students are stressed. We have evidence now that suggests strongly that timed math tests in the early grades are responsible for the early onset of math anxiety for many students. I teach an undergraduate class at Stanford, and many of the undergraduates are math traumatized. When I ask them what happened to cause this, almost all of them will recall, with startling clarity, the time in elementary school when they were given timed tests. We are really pleased that "Fluency without Fear" has now been used across the United States to pull timed tests out of school districts. It has been downloaded many thousands of times and used in state and national hearings.

One of the reasons for the amazing success of the paper is that it does not just share the brain science on the damage of timed tests but also offers an alternative to timed tests: activities that teach math facts conceptually and through activities that students and teachers enjoy. One of the activities—a game called How Close to 100—became so popular that thousands of teachers tweeted photos of their students playing the game. There was so much attention on Twitter and other media that Stanford noticed and decided to write a news story on the damage of speed to mathematics learning. This was picked up by news outlets across the United States, including *US News & World Report,* which is part of the reason the white paper has now had so many downloads and so much impact. Teachers themselves caused this mini revolution by spreading news of the activities and research.

How Close to 100 is just one of many tasks we have on youcubed.org that are extremely popular with teachers and students. All our tasks have the feature of being "low floor and high ceiling," which I consider to be an extremely important quality for engaging all students in a class. If you are teaching only one student, then a mathematics task can be fairly narrow in terms of its content and difficulty. But whenever you have a group of students, there will be differences in their needs, and they will be challenged by different ideas. A low-floor, high-ceiling task is one in which everyone can engage, no matter what his or her prior understanding or knowledge, but also one that is open enough to extend to high levels, so that all students can be deeply challenged. In the last two years, we have launched an introductory week of mathematics lessons on our site that are open, visual, and low floor, high ceiling. These have been extremely popular with teachers; they have had approximately four million downloads and are used in 20% of schools across the United States.

In our extensive work with teachers around the United States, we are continually asked for more tasks that are like those on our website. Most textbook publishers seem to ignore or be unaware of research on mathematics learning, and most textbook questions are narrow and insufficiently engaging for students. It is imperative that the new knowledge of the ways our brains learn mathematics is incorporated into the lessons students are given in classrooms. It is for this reason that we chose to write a series of books that are organized around a principle of active student engagement, that reflect the latest brain science on learning, and that include activities that are low floor and high ceiling.

Youcubed Summer Camp

We recently brought 81 students onto the Stanford campus for a Youcubed summer math camp, to teach them in the ways that are encouraged in this book. We used open, creative, and visual math tasks. After only 18 lessons with us, the students improved their test score performance by an average of 50%, the equivalent of 1.6 years of school. More important, they changed their relationship with mathematics and started believing in their own potential. They did this, in part, because we talked to them about the brain science showing that

- There is no such thing as a math person—anyone can learn mathematics to high levels.
- Mistakes, struggle, and challenge are critical for brain growth.
- Speed is unimportant in mathematics.
- Mathematics is a visual and beautiful subject, and our brains want to think visually about mathematics.

All of these messages were key to the students' changed mathematics relationship, but just as critical were the tasks we worked on in class. The tasks and the messages about the brain were perfect complements to each other, as we told students they could learn anything, and we showed them a mathematics that was open, creative, and engaging. This approach helped them see that they could learn mathematics and actually do so. This book shares the kinds of tasks that we used in our summer camp, that make up our week of inspirational mathematics (WIM) lessons, and that we post on our site.

Before I outline and introduce the different sections of the book and the ways we are choosing to engage students, I will share some important ideas about how students learn mathematics.

Memorization versus Conceptual Engagement

Many students get the wrong idea about mathematics—exactly the wrong idea. Through years of mathematics classes, many students come to believe that their role in mathematics learning is to memorize methods and facts, and that mathematics success comes from memorization. I say this is exactly the wrong idea because there is actually very little to remember in mathematics. The subject is made up of a few big, linked ideas, and students who are successful in mathematics are those who see the subject as a set of ideas that they need to think deeply about. The Program for International Student Assessment (PISA) tests are international assessments of mathematics, reading, and science that are given every three years. In 2012, PISA not only assessed mathematics achievement but also collected data on students' approach to mathematics. I worked with the PISA team in Paris at the Organisation for Economic Co-operation and Development (OECD) to analyze students' mathematics approaches and their relationship to achievement. One clear result emerged from this analysis. Students approached mathematics in three distinct ways. One group approached mathematics by attempting to memorize the methods they had met; another group took a "relational" approach, relating new concepts to those they already knew; and a third group took a self-monitoring approach, thinking about what they knew and needed to know.

In every country, the memorizers were the lowest-achieving students, and countries with high numbers of memorizers were all lower achieving. In no country were memorizers in the highest-achieving group, and in some high-achieving countries such as Japan, students who combined self-monitoring and relational strategies outscored memorizing students by more than a year's worth of schooling. More detail on this finding is given in this *Scientific American* Mind article that I coauthored with a PISA analyst: https://www.scientificamerican.com/article/why-math-education-in-the-u-s-doesn-t-add-up/.

Mathematics is a conceptual subject, and it is important for students to be thinking slowly, deeply, and conceptually about mathematical ideas, not racing through methods that they try to memorize. One reason that students need to think conceptually has to do with the ways the brain processes mathematics. When we learn new mathematical ideas, they take up a large space in our brain as the brain works out where they fit and what they connect with. But with time, as we move on with our understanding, the knowledge becomes compressed in the brain, taking up a very small space. For first graders, the idea of addition takes up a large space in their brains as they think about how it works and what it means, but for adults the idea of addition is compressed, and it takes up a small space. When adults are asked to add 2 and 3, for example, they can quickly and easily extract the compressed knowledge. William Thurston (1990), a mathematician who won the Field's Medal—the highest honor in mathematics—explains compression like this:

> Mathematics is amazingly compressible: you may struggle a long time, step by step, to work through the same process or idea from several approaches. But once you really understand it and have the mental perspective to see it as a whole, there is often a tremendous mental compression. You can file it away, recall it quickly and completely when you need it, and use it as just one step in some other mental process. The insight that goes with this compression is one of the real joys of mathematics.

You will probably agree with me that not many students think of mathematics as a "real joy," and part of the reason is that they are not compressing mathematical ideas in their brain. This is because the brain only compresses concepts, not methods. So if students are thinking that mathematics is a set of methods to memorize, they are on the wrong pathway, and it is critical that we change that. It is very important that students think deeply and conceptually about ideas. We provide the activities in this book that will allow students to think deeply and conceptually, and an essential role of the teacher is to give the students time to do so.

Mathematical Thinking, Reasoning, and Convincing

When we worked with our Youcubed camp students, we gave each of them journals to record their mathematical thinking. I am a big fan of journaling—for myself and my students. For mathematics students, it helps show them that mathematics is a subject for which we should record ideas and pictures. We can use journaling to encourage students to keep organized records, which is another important part of mathematics, and help them understand that mathematical thinking can be a long and slow process. Journals also give students free space—where they can be creative, share ideas, and feel ownership of their work. We did not write in the students' journals, as we wanted them to think of the journals as their space, not something that teachers wrote on. We gave students feedback on sticky notes that we stuck onto their work. The images in Figure I.1 show some of the mathematical records the camp students kept in their journals.

Another resource I always share with learners is the act of color coding—that is, students using colors to highlight different ideas. For example, when working on an algebraic task, they may show the *x* in the same color in an expression, in a graph, and in a picture, as shown in Figure I.2. When adding numbers, color coding may help show the addends (Figure I.3).

Color coding highlights connections, which are a really critical part of mathematics.

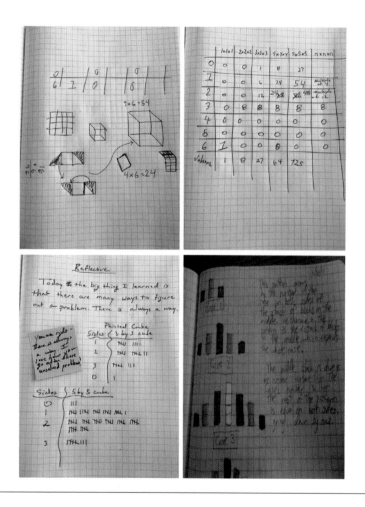

Figure I.1

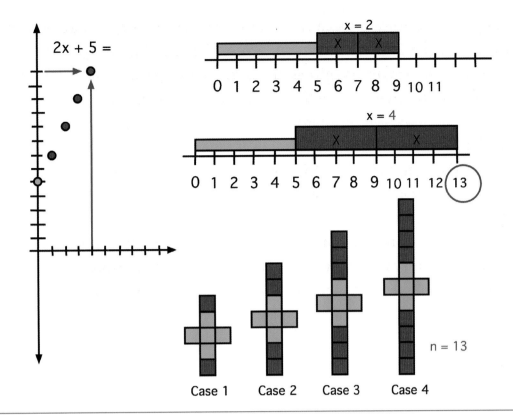

Figure I.2

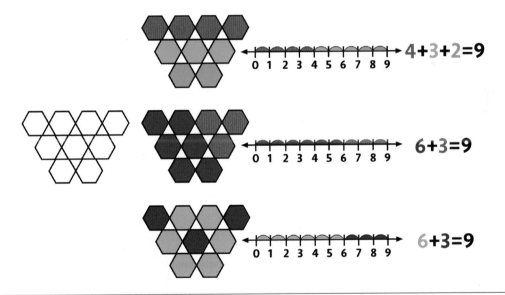

Figure I.3

Another important part of mathematics is the act of reasoning—explaining why methods are chosen and how steps are linked, and using logic to connect ideas. Reasoning is at the heart of mathematics. Scientists prove ideas by finding more cases that fit a theory, or countercases that contradict a theory, but mathematicians prove their work by reasoning. If students are not reasoning, then they are not really doing mathematics. In the activities of these books, we suggest a framework that encourages students to be convincing when they reason. We tell them that there are three levels of being convincing. The first, or easiest, level is to convince yourself of something. A higher level is to convince a friend. And the highest level of all is to convince a skeptic. We also share with students that they should be skeptics with one another, asking one another why methods were chosen and how they work. We have found this framework to be very powerful with students; they enjoy being skeptics, pushing each other to deeper levels of reasoning, and it encourages students to reason clearly, which is important for their learning.

We start each book in our series with an activity that invites students to reason about mathematics and be convincing. I first met an activity like this when reading Mark Driscoll's teaching ideas in his book *Fostering Algebraic Thinking.* I thought it was a perfect activity for introducing the skeptics framework that I had learned from a wonderful teacher, Cathy Humphreys. She had learned about and adapted the framework from two of my inspirational teachers from England: mathematician John Mason and mathematics educator Leone Burton. As well as encouraging students to be convincing, in a number of activities we ask students to prove an idea. Some people think of proof as a formal set of steps that they learned in geometry class. But the act of proving is really about connecting ideas, and as students enter the learning journey of proving, it is worthwhile celebrating their steps toward formal proof. Mathematician Paul Lockhart (2012) rejects the idea that proving is about following a set of formal steps, instead proposing that proving is "abstract art, pure and simple. And art is always a struggle. There is no systematic way of creating beautiful and meaningful paintings or sculptures, and there is also no method for producing beautiful and meaningful mathematical arguments" (p. 8). Instead of suggesting that students follow formal steps, we invite them to think deeply about mathematical concepts and make connections. Students will be given many ways to be creative when they prove and justify, and for reasons I discuss later, we always encourage and celebrate visual as well as numerical and algebraic justifications. Ideally, students will create visual, numerical, and algebraic representations and connect their ideas through color coding and through verbal explanations. Students are excited to experience mathematics in these ways, and they benefit from the opportunity to bring their individual ideas and creativity to the problem-solving and learning space. As students develop in their mathematical understanding, we can encourage them to extend and generalize their ideas through reasoning, justifying, and proving. This process deepens their understanding and helps them compress their learning.

Big Ideas

The books in the Mindset Mathematics Series are all organized around mathematical "big ideas." Mathematics is not a set of methods; it is a set of connected ideas that need to be understood. When students understand the big ideas in mathematics, the methods and rules fall into place. One of the reasons any set of curriculum standards is flawed is that standards take the beautiful subject of mathematics and its many connections, and divide it into small pieces that make the connections disappear. Instead of starting with the small pieces, we have started with the big ideas and important connections, and have listed the relevant Common Core curriculum standards within the activities. Our activities invite students to engage in the mathematical acts that are listed in the imperative Common Core practice standards, and they also teach many of the Common Core content standards, which emerge from the rich activities. Student activity pages are noted with a ⬙ and teacher activity pages are noted with a ▭.

Although we have chapters for each big idea, as though they are separate from each other, they are all intrinsically linked. Figure I.4 shows some of the connections between the ideas, and you may be able to see others. It is very important to share with students that mathematics is a subject of connections and to highlight the connections as students work. You may want to print the color visual of the different connections for students to see as they work. To see the maps of big ideas for all of the grades K through 8, find our paper "What Is Mathematical Beauty?" at youcubed.org.

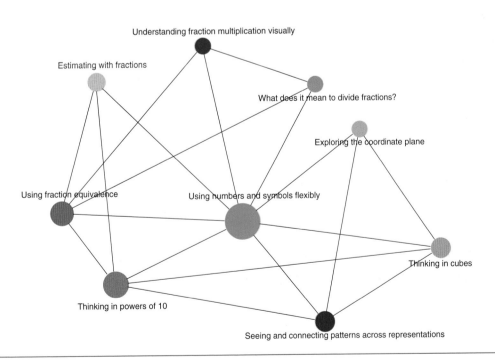

Figure I.4

Structure of the Book

Visualize. Play. Investigate. These three words provide the structure for each book in the series. They also pave the way for open student thinking, for powerful brain connections, for engagement, and for deep understanding. How do they do that? And why is this book so different from other mathematics curriculum books?

Visualize 🌀

For the past few years, I have been working with a neuroscience group at Stanford, under the direction of Vinod Menon, which specializes in mathematics learning. We have been working together to think about the ways that findings from brain science can be used to help learners of mathematics. One of the exciting discoveries that has been emerging over the last few years is the importance of visualizing for the brain and our learning of mathematics. Brain scientists now know that when we work on mathematics, even when we perform a bare number calculation, five areas of the brain are involved, as shown in Figure I.5.

Two of the five brain pathways—the dorsal and ventral pathways—are visual. The dorsal visual pathway is the main brain region for representing quantity. This may seem

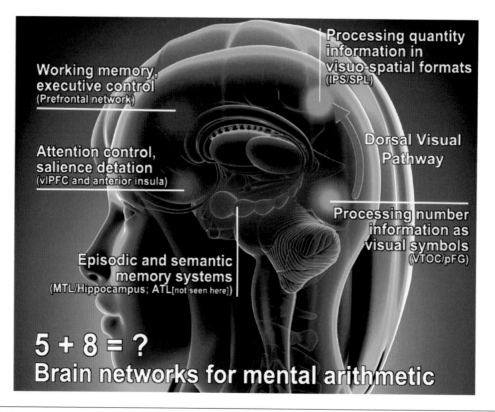

Figure I.5

surprising, as so many of us have sat through hundreds of hours of mathematics classes working with numbers, while barely ever engaging visually with mathematics. Now brain scientists know that our brains "see" fingers when we calculate, and knowing fingers well—what they call finger perception—is critical for the development of an understanding of number. If you would like to read more about the importance of finger work in mathematics, look at the visual mathematics section of youcubed.org. Number lines are really helpful, as they provide the brain with a visual representation of number order. In one study, a mere four 15-minute sessions of students playing with a number line completely eradicated the differences between students from low-income and middle-income backgrounds coming into school (Siegler & Ramani, 2008).

Our brain wants to think visually about mathematics, yet few curriculum materials engage students in visual thinking. Some mathematics books show pictures, but they rarely ever invite students to do their own visualizing and drawing. The neuroscientists' research shows the importance not only of visual thinking but also of students' connecting different areas of their brains as they work on mathematics. The scientists now know that as children learn and develop, they increase the connections between different parts of the brain, and they particularly develop connections between symbolic and visual representations of numbers. Increased mathematics achievement comes about when students are developing those connections. For so long, our emphasis in mathematics education has been on symbolic representations of numbers, with students developing one area of the brain that is concerned with symbolic number representation. A more productive and engaging approach is to develop all areas of the brain that are involved in mathematical thinking, and visual connections are critical to this development.

In addition to the brain development that occurs when students think visually, we have found that visual activities are really engaging for students. Even students who think they are "not visual learners" (an incorrect idea) become fascinated and think deeply about mathematics that is shown visually—such as the visual representations of the calculation 18×5 shown in Figure I.6.

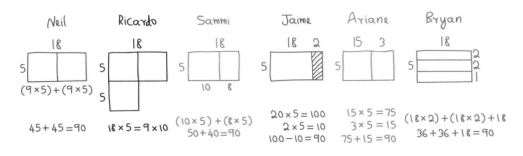

Figure I.6

In our Youcubed teaching of summer school to sixth- and seventh-grade students and in our trialing of Youcubed's WIM materials, we have found that students are inspired by the creativity that is possible when mathematics is visual. When we were trialing the materials in a local middle school one day, a parent stopped me and asked what we had been doing. She said that her daughter had always said she hated and couldn't do math, but after working on our tasks, she came home saying she could see a future for herself in mathematics. We had been working on the number visuals that we use throughout these teaching materials, shown in Figure I.7.

The parent reported that when her daughter had seen the creativity possible in mathematics, everything had changed for her. I strongly believe that we can give these insights and inspirations to many more learners with the sort of creative, open mathematics tasks that fill this book.

We have also found that when we present visual activities to students, the status differences that often get in the way of good mathematics teaching disappear. I was visiting a first-grade classroom recently, and the teacher had set up four different stations around the room. In all of them, the students were working on arithmetic. In one, the teacher engaged students in a mini number talk; in another, a teaching

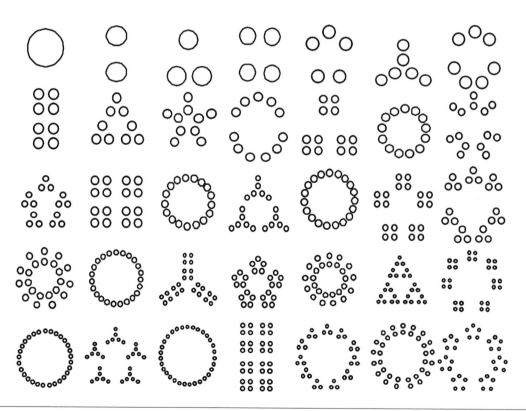

Figure I.7

Mindset Mathematics, Grade 5

assistant worked on an activity with coins; in the third, the students played a board game; and in the fourth, they worked on a number worksheet. In each of the first three stations, the students collaborated and worked really well, but as soon as students went to the worksheet station, conversations changed, and in every group I heard statements like "This is easy," " I've finished," "I can't do this," and "Haven't you finished yet?" These status comments are unfortunate and off-putting for many students. I now try to present mathematical tasks without numbers as often as possible, or I take out the calculation part of a task, as it is the numerical and calculational aspects that often cause students to feel less sure of themselves. This doesn't mean that students cannot have a wonderful and productive relationship with numbers, as we hope to promote in this book, but sometimes the key mathematical idea can be arrived at without any numbers at all.

Almost all the tasks in our book invite students to think visually about mathematics and to connect visual and numerical representations. This encourages important brain connections as well as deep student engagement.

Play

The key to reducing status differences in mathematics classrooms, in my view, comes from *opening* mathematics. When we teach students that we can see or approach any mathematical idea in different ways, they start to respect the different thinking of all students. Opening mathematics involves inviting students to see ideas differently, explore with ideas, and ask their own questions. Students can gain access to the same mathematical ideas and methods through creativity and exploration that they can by being taught methods that they practice. As well as reducing or removing status differences, open mathematics is more engaging for students. This is why we are inviting students, through these mathematics materials, to play with mathematics. Albert Einstein famously once said that "play is the highest form of research." This is because play is an opportunity for ideas to be used and developed in the service of something enjoyable. In the Play activities of our materials, students are invited to work with an important idea in a free space where they can enjoy the freedom of mathematical play. This does not mean that the activities do not teach essential mathematical content and practices—they do, as they invite students to work with the ideas. We have designed the Play activities to downplay competition and instead invite students to work with each other, building understanding together.

Investigate ❓

Our Investigate activities add something very important: they give students opportunities to take ideas to the sky. They also have a playful element, but the difference is that they pose questions that students can explore and take to very high levels. As I mentioned earlier, all of our tasks are designed to be as low floor and high ceiling as possible, as these provide the best conditions for engaging all students, whatever their prior knowledge. Any student can access them, and students can take the ideas to high levels. We should always be open to being surprised by what our learners can do, and always provide all students with opportunities to take work to high levels and to be challenged.

A crucial finding from neuroscience is the importance of students struggling and making mistakes—these are the times when brains grow the most. In one of my meetings with a leading neuroscientist, he stated it very clearly: if students are not struggling, they are not learning. We want to put students into situations where they feel that work is hard, but within their reach. Do not worry if students ask questions that you don't know the answer to; that is a good thing. One of the damaging ideas that teachers and students share in education is that teachers of mathematics know everything. This gives students the idea that mathematics people are those who know a lot and never make mistakes, which is an incorrect and harmful message. It is good to say to your students, "That is a great question that we can all think about" or "I have never thought about that idea; let's investigate it together." It is even good to make mistakes in front of students, as it shows them that mistakes are an important part of mathematical work. As they investigate, they should be going to places you have never thought about—taking ideas in new directions and exploring uncharted territory. Model for students what it means to be a curious mathematics learner, always open to learning new ideas and being challenged yourself.

* * *

We have designed activities to take at least a class period, but some of them could go longer, especially if students ask deep questions or start an investigation into a cool idea. If you can be flexible about students' time on activities, that is ideal, or you may wish to suggest that students continue activities at home. In our teaching of these activities, we have found that students are so excited by the ideas that they take them home to their families and continue working on them, which is wonderful. At all times, celebrate deep thinking over speed, as that is the nature of real mathematical thought. Ask students to come up with creative representations of their ideas; celebrate their drawing, modeling, and any form of creativity. Invite your students into a journey of mathematical curiosity and take that journey with them, walking by their side as they experience the wonder of open, mindset mathematics.

References

Lockhart, P. (2012). *Measurement.* Cambridge, MA: Harvard University Press.

Siegler, R. S., & Ramani, G. B. (2008). Playing linear numerical board games promotes low income children's numerical development. *Developmental Science, 11*(5), 655–661. doi:10.1111/j.1467-7687.2008.00714.x

Thurston, W. (1990). Mathematical education. *Notices of the American Mathematical Society, 37*(7), 844–850.

Activities for Building Norms

Encouraging Good Group Work

We always use this activity before students work on math together, as it helps improve group interactions. Teachers who have tried this activity have been pleased by students' thoughtful responses and found the students' thoughts and words helpful in creating a positive and supportive environment. The first thing to do is to ask students, in groups, to reflect on things they don't like people to say or do in a group when they are working on math together. Students come up with quite a few important ideas, such as not liking people to give away the answer, to rush through the work, or to ignore other people's ideas. When students have had enough time in groups brainstorming, collect the ideas. We usually do this by making a What We Don't Like list or poster and asking each group to contribute one idea, moving around the room until a few good ideas have been shared (usually about 10). Then we do the same for the What We Do Like list or poster. It can be good to present the final posters to the class as the agreed-on classroom norms that you and they can reflect back on over the year. If any student shares a negative comment, such as "I don't like waiting for slow people," do not put it on the poster; instead use it as a chance to discuss the issue. This rarely happens, and students are usually very thoughtful and respectful in the ideas they share.

Activity	Time	Description/Prompt	Materials
Launch	5 min	Explain to students that working in groups is an important part of what mathematicians do. Mathematicians discuss their ideas and work together to solve challenging problems. It's important to work together, and we need to discuss what helps us work well together.	
Explore	10 min	Assign a group facilitator to make sure that all students get to share their thoughts on points 1 and 2. Groups should record every group member's ideas and then decide which they will share during the whole-class discussion. In your groups . . . 1. Reflect on the things you do not like people to say or do when you are working on math together in a group. 2. Reflect on the things you do like people to say or do when you are working on math together in a group.	• Paper • Pencil or pen
Discuss	10 min	Ask each group to share their findings. Condense their responses and make a poster so that the student ideas are visible and you can refer to them during the class.	Two to four pieces of large poster paper to collect the students' ideas

Paper Folding: Learning to Reason, Convince, and Be Skeptical

Connection to CCSS
5.G.3
5.G.4

One of the most important topics in mathematics is reasoning. Whereas scientists prove or disprove ideas by finding cases, mathematicians prove their ideas by reasoning—making logical connections between ideas. This activity gives students an opportunity to learn to reason well by having to convince others who are being skeptical.

Before beginning the activity, explain to students that their role is to be convincing. The easiest person to convince is yourself. A higher level of being convincing is to convince a friend, and the highest level of all is to convince a skeptic. In this activity, the students learn to reason to the extent that they can convince a skeptic. Students should work in pairs and take turns to be the one convincing and the one being a skeptic.

Give each student a square piece of paper. If you already have 8.5×11 paper, you can ask them to make the square first.

The first challenge is for one of the students to fold the paper to make a scalene triangle that does not include any of the edges of the paper. She should convince her partner that it is a scalene triangle, using what she knows about triangles to be convincing. The skeptic partner should ask lots of skeptical questions, such as "How do you know that all sides are a different length?" and not accept that they are because it looks like they are.

The partners should then switch roles, and the other student folds the paper into a trapezoid that does not include any of the edges of the paper. His partner should be skeptical and push for high levels of reasoning.

The partners should then switch again, and the challenge is to fold the paper to make a rhombus, again not using the edges of the paper.

The fourth challenge is to make a different rhombus. For each challenge, partners must reason and be skeptical.

When the task is complete, facilitate a whole-class discussion in which students discuss the following questions:

- Which was the most challenging task? Why?
- What was hard about reasoning and being convincing?
- What was hard about being a skeptic?

Activity	Time	Description/Prompt	Materials
Launch	5 min	Tell students that their role for the day is to be convincing and to be a skeptic. Ask students to fold a piece of paper into a square. Choose a student and model being a skeptic.	
Explore	10 min	Show students the task and explain that in each round, they are to solve the folding problem. In pairs, students alternate folding and reasoning and being the skeptic. After students convince themselves they have solved each problem, they switch roles and fold the next challenge. Give students square paper or ask them to start by making a square. The convincing challenges are as follows: 1. Fold your paper into a scalene triangle that does not include any edges of the paper. 2. Fold your paper into a trapezoid that does not include any edges of the paper. 3. Fold your paper into an rhombus that does not include any edges of the paper. 4. Fold your paper into a different rhombus that does not include any edges of the paper.	• One piece of 8.5" × 11" paper per student • Paper Folding worksheet for each student
Discuss	10 min	Discuss the activity as a class. Make sure to discuss the roles of convincer and skeptic.	

Paper Folding: Learning to Reason, Convince, and Be a Skeptic

1. Fold your paper into a scalene triangle that does not include any edges of the paper. Convince a skeptic that it is a triangle.
   Reflection:

   Switch roles

2. Fold your paper into a trapezoid that does not include any edges of the paper. Convince a skeptic that it is a trapezoid.
   Reflection:

   Switch roles

3. Fold your paper into a rhombus that does not include any edges of the paper. Convince a skeptic that it is a rhombus.
   Reflection:

   Switch roles

4. Fold your paper into a different rhombus that does not include any edges of the paper. Convince a skeptic that it is a rhombus.
   Reflection:

BIG IDEA 1

Thinking in Cubes

The new brain science shows that five different pathways are involved when people think about mathematical ideas, and two of these are visual. When we make mathematics visual for students, we help them learn and hold ideas in powerful ways in their brains, as the introduction to this book explains. Similarly, we now know that movement really helps with mathematical ideas and is important for brain development. When students move with mathematics, it means that the mathematical ideas are held in the sensory-motor portions of the brain, which helps students understand the ideas powerfully. We see evidence of people holding mathematical ideas in these parts of their brains when they gesture to illustrate an idea; when people talk about circles, for example, they often draw a circle in the air. This big idea gives students opportunities to touch and feel mathematical ideas, and that is meaningful to students of any age.

In our Visualize activity, students will build with cubes and develop connections between two- and three-dimensional representations of solids. They will be asked to think about the outside and inside of cubes, which is important geometric thinking. As they physically model and also draw, they will build significant brain connections.

In the Play activity, students will construct cities of cubes that match views that we give them, again using brain pathways that will develop mathematical thinking. Students also will build their own cities, which will be engaging and exciting for them, enhancing the learning potential of the activities. As students think visually and also bring in numerical thinking, their brains will develop pathways between the areas that are used for these different types of thinking.

In our Investigate activity, students will again have the opportunity to feel cubes and consider their size physically and with numbers, encouraging brain connections. They also get to work with some constraints that will guide their thinking and learning. Students will be asked to investigate the volume of rectangular solids by packing little boxes into larger boxes of their own design. Any time that students are asked to bring their own ideas into mathematics, such as when they make their own designs, they are working with agency, which will help them enjoy mathematics and also see it as an active subject that they should think deeply about. When students work with agency, their work is closer to that of a mathematician, and inviting students to combine their own ideas with formal mathematical ideas is a really worthwhile goal. The activities that make up this big idea provide plenty of opportunities for students to combine their own thinking with major mathematical ideas and principles.

Jo Boaler

Solids, Inside and Out

Snapshot

Students build connections between two- and three-dimensional representations of solids by using views of a rectangular solid to construct a model with cubes. Students investigate what the inside looks like and compare results.

Connection to CCSS
5.MD.3
5.MD.4

Agenda

Activity	Time	Description/Prompt	Materials
Launch	5 min	Show students the two-dimensional views of a rectangular solid constructed out of 60 cubes. Challenge students to build this solid.	Rectangular Solids Sheet, to display for the class
Explore	30 min	Partnerships try to build a rectangular solid from 60 cubes so that it matches the views provided. Students then consider what the inside looks like and figure out how to construct and draw a model of the cubes that cannot be seen.	• Rectangular Solids Sheets, one per partnership • Snap or multilink cubes for each partnership: 15 each of red, green, yellow, and blue • Drawing Solids Sheet, one per partnership
Discuss	20 min	Students compare their results and discuss how they used the views to construct the solid. Students discuss the differences between their models of the inside.	

(*Continued*)

Activity	Time	Description/Prompt	Materials
Extend	30–60 min	Partnerships construct their own rectangular solid puzzles and swap with other groups to solve.	• Drawing Solids Sheet, at least one per partnership • Cubes • Colors • Baskets, trays, or bags for students' puzzles

To the Teacher

Students often struggle when moving between two-dimensional representations of solids objects, like the ones shown in Figure 1.1, and three-dimensional representations. Two-dimensional drawings of solids force us to imagine the parts we cannot see, and students need experiences with mentally rotating and imagining these invisible parts. Similarly, we often encounter multiple views of three-dimensional objects aimed at helping us see what one view does not show. These offer a different challenge: constructing the three-dimensional whole from parts. In this visual activity, students are asked to move repeatedly between two-dimensional and three-dimensional representations to build connections and a deeper sense of what it means to be solid.

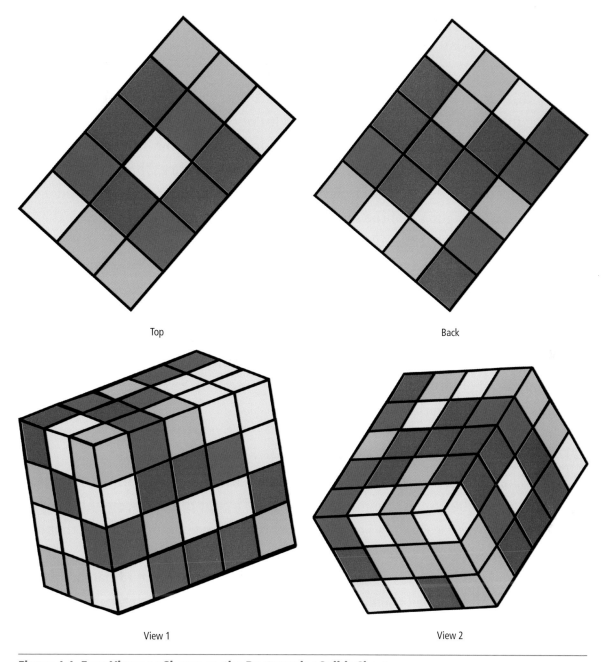

Top   Back

View 1   View 2

Figure 1.1 Four Views as Shown on the Rectangular Solids Sheet

The extension activity pushes these connections even further by asking students to create and draw their own solids and then try to build solids designed by others. This extension could easily take another full day or more, depending on how excited students are. They may want to construct multiple puzzles and solve many as well. We encourage you to follow students' interests and allow as much time as students want for constructing puzzles. The repeated engagement with building, drawing, and mentally manipulating the solids will help develop important ways of thinking about solids and volume for future work.

Activity

Launch

Launch this lesson by telling students that we are going to be exploring ways to fill space. In the past, they have likely spent a lot of time thinking about how to cover two-dimensional shapes with squares to find the area, but now we are going to think about how to fill three-dimensional solids with cubes. Show students the views provided on the Rectangular Solid Sheet shown in Figure 1.1. Tell students that all of these images are of the same rectangular solid, and each image is called a *view*. Tell students that the solid is made of 60 blocks: 15 are red, 15 are green, 15 are yellow, and 15 are blue. Their challenge today is to build this solid. Partners will each get a copy of the views and enough blocks to construct the solid. If you are not able to copy the Rectangular Solid Sheet in color for students, we suggest you display the images in color using a projector and provide students with the blank version, which they can color in themselves. Coloring in the individual cubes may also help students attend their arrangement on each face and support students with building the solid.

Explore

Have students work in partnerships. Provide each partnership with 15 red, 15 green, 15 yellow, and 15 blue snap or multilink cubes, and a copy of the Rectangular Solid Sheet. Partnerships use the views to try to construct the rectangular solid so that it matches the views.

After students have built the solid and both partners agree that it matches the views and uses all 60 cubes, then challenge students to figure out what cubes are on the inside. Ask, What cubes are we not able see? Can you make a model of what is inside your solid? Provide partners with additional cubes and a copy of the Drawing Solids Sheet. Ask them to draw an image of what is inside their solid once they have built their model.

Discuss

Bring students together with their models of the rectangular solid, models of the inside, and drawings of the inside. Pair partnerships up to share their two models and drawings, as in a turn and talk. Then bring all students together to discuss the following questions:

- How did you figure out how to build your solid? What did you have to think about?
- How did you use the images to help you?
- What was hard about building the rectangular solid so that it matched the views you were given?
- What did you notice when you compared your models to those others made?

Then discuss the models of the inside of the solid:

- What was inside your solid? How did you figure it out?
- How are the insides of our solids similar? Different? Why?

Extend

Invite students to create their own rectangular solid puzzle for another partnership to solve. Provide students with additional copies of the Drawing Solids Sheet, colors, and a container for their puzzle. Students should first use any number of their cubes to build a rectangular solid. They then use their solid to construct multiple views of it on a copy of the Drawing Solids Sheet. Push students to think carefully about which views they will show so that it is challenging but possible to build the solid with the views they provide. Once they are confident that their views are accurate, ask students to deconstruct their solid and place their views and cubes into a container (basket, tray, or bag). You may want to ask students to name their puzzle or put their names on it. Then students can trade puzzles with another group and try to build their solid. After students have spent some time exploring one another's puzzles, you may want to bring them back together to discuss questions like these:

- What makes a good puzzle?
- What made solving a rectangular solid puzzle easier or harder?
- What strategies for solving these puzzles have you and your partner come up with?

Look-Fors

- **Are students creating a solid?** Students may be tempted to construct only what they see in the images and presume that there is nothing inside the solid at all. Challenge students who have leftover cubes by asking: Is your solid constructed with 60 cubes? Why not? Does it match the views you were given? How can you make your solid meet all of the constraints of the problem?

- **How are students mentally rotating the images?** Students may struggle to mentally manipulate the images provided to figure out how the pieces fit together. Often students don't realize that rotating the paper can help them see the images differently. Some students may be overwhelmed by the images and not know how to get started. Consider prompting students by asking: Is there one image that makes sense to you? How could you get started with that one image and then see how it fits with the others? What could you do with your paper to help you see how the pieces fit together?

- **How are students interpreting the images?** Drawing a three-dimensional object on two-dimensional paper is a challenge. If students have not yet had experience with isometric dot paper (see appendix), you may want to ask them to try drawing a single cube first, just to explore how the dot paper works. You might also ask them to think about the views they were provided and how they could use those as models.

Reflect

What surprised you about building rectangular solids from cubes and views?

Rectangular Solids Sheet

Use 15 yellow, 15 red, 15 blue, and 15 green cubes to build the rectangular solid.

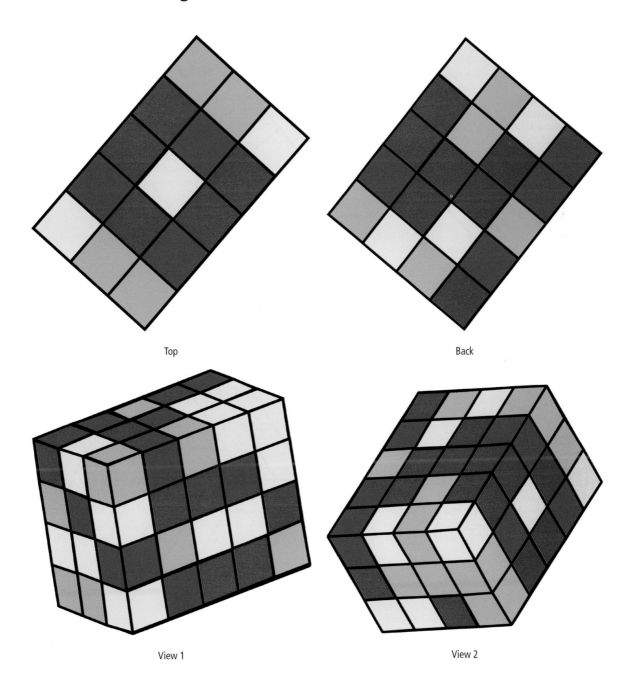

Top

Back

View 1

View 2

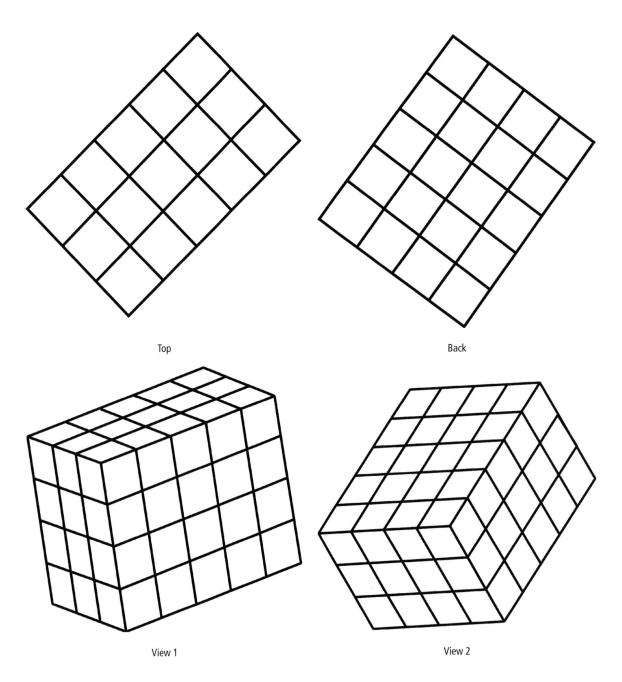

Top

Back

View 1

View 2

City of Cubes
Snapshot

Students use multiple views of block towers to construct cities of cubes that match those views. Students learn that the number of cubes used to build the city is its volume, and develop their own City of Cubes puzzles, which support students in learning how to record complex three-dimensional figures on paper and interpret those representations.

Connection to CCSS
5.MD.3
5.MD.4,
5.MD.5c

Agenda

Activity	Time	Description/Prompt	Materials
Launch	5–10 min	Show students examples of architectural images and discuss what they communicate. Show students similar views from a City of Cubes puzzle and make sure students understand what is shown.	• Architectural Drawing sheets • Views from the first City of Cubes Puzzle sheet
Play	30+ min	Students work in partners to try to build the City of Cube puzzles from different sets of views. Students explore whether more than one city is possible and how many cubes it would take to build those cities.	• All three City of Cubes Puzzle sheets, copied for partners to choose • Snap, multilink, or uni-fix cubes in multiple colors, for all partnerships • Isometric dot and grid paper (see appendix)
Discuss	15 min	Discuss the strategies students used for solving the puzzles and the multiple possible solutions they developed.	• Student-built City of Cubes puzzles

(Continued)

Activity	Time	Description/Prompt	Materials
Play	30+ min	Partners work together to design their own City of Cubes puzzles. Then partnerships swap puzzles, solve each other's, share solutions, and offer feedback for improving the puzzles.	• Snap, multilink, or uni-fix cubes in multiple colors, for all partnerships • Isometric dot and grid paper (see appendix) • Colors
Discuss	15 min	Discuss the challenges of creating these puzzles and what students learned from the cycles of solving, sharing, and giving and receiving feedback.	

To the Teacher

The City of Cubes views we have provided use multiple colors to support students in making sense of the images. Each tower uses a single color of cubes. You may not have the same color cubes as indicated in our drawings. Provide students with whatever colors you have available and tell students that they can represent the towers in whatever colors they choose. Changing the colors, though, will likely make moving between the views and their own work a bit more difficult. You may want to encourage students to jot down on the views which colors they are using for each tower to help them track their own work.

In the second half of this lesson, we give students the opportunity to create their own puzzles. Recording a three-dimensional figure on paper is quite different from interpreting a set of drawings to build a figure. Students need opportunities to engage with both activities, and each will challenge students in different ways. Remind students how important it is to feel challenged and to work on mathematical ideas that allow them to struggle. We anticipate that this lesson will take more than one day. After the lesson, you may also want to incorporate students' puzzles into stations or games for indoor recess.

Activity

Launch

Launch the lesson by showing students some images of architectural drawings that architects produce to communicate what the buildings they design might look like (Figure 1.2). They often create floor plans that show what each floor looks like from above, and they make views of the outside so that you can see how buildings look in relationship to each other.

Front and Side View
Source: Shutterstock.com/paparoma

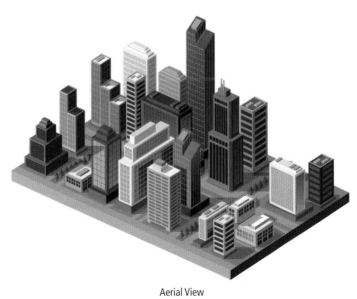

Aerial View
Source: Shutterstock.com/bioraven

Figure 1.2 Architectural Drawings

Tell students that today they are going to use some images of cube cities to try to build what is shown. Show students an example of the views from the first City of Cubes puzzle. Show students the aerial view and be sure they understand it as how the city might look from a helicopter looking straight down. Show students side views and be sure they understand these as what they would see standing on the outside looking at the city. You may want to give students a moment to turn and talk to a partner about what they notice in these images, then collect some observations. Ask, Can you build this city using these views?

Play

Invite partners to choose one of the three City of Cubes puzzles to try to build first. Students should have access to colored cubes to build each city. For each city they build, students try to figure out the following:

- How many cubes could it take to build this city?
- Is there more than one way to build a city that matches the views given?
- If there is more than one way, what is the fewest number of cubes it could take to build it? What is the greatest number of cubes you could use to build it?

Students should document their findings, either by saving the models they construct (if you have enough cubes) or by devising a way of recording on paper the possibilities they create. Provide isometric dot paper or grid paper (see appendix) for those who would like these tools.

Discuss

When students have had a chance to fully explore at least one of these puzzles, gather students together with their evidence (models or drawings) to discuss the following questions:

- How did you tackle building the cities? What strategies were useful? How did you use the colors?
- How many cubes did it take to build each city? How do you know?
- Which cities can be built in more than one way? What is the fewest number of cubes it could take to build the city? What is the greatest? How do you know?

During this discussion, name the number of cubes needed to construct the city as its *volume.* At the close of the discussion, challenge students to create their own City of Cubes puzzles.

Play

Partners work to create their own City of Cubes puzzle(s). Encourage students to build their cities and then use their buildings to create images on grid and/or dot paper (see appendix) that they could give to others as a puzzle. Remind students how colors help them make sense of the images, and ask students to use color in their puzzle drawings. Students should consider what views they want to provide and whether they want their puzzle to have multiple solutions.

When partnerships have finished creating a puzzle, they can swap with other partners and try their puzzles. For each puzzle students try, ask them to consider the following:

- What could the volume be?
- Are there multiple possible cities that match the views you were given?
- Do you have suggestions for the puzzle creators for how to make the puzzle clearer or more interesting?

After students swap, they can return the puzzle to its creators, share solutions, and provide some feedback on how to make the puzzle clearer or more interesting. Swapping, solving, and sharing rounds can be repeated as long as students are engaged.

Discuss

After the class has had a chance to create, swap, and share results from their puzzles, gather students together for one final discussion:

- What was challenging about making your own? What was challenging about creating the drawings? How did you address these challenges?
- What makes a city hard to build? What images make it easier to build?
- What strategies did you use?
- How did you figure out the volume of the city?
- What feedback did you receive that was most useful for improving your puzzle? Why was it helpful?

Look-Fors

- **How are students interpreting the two-dimensional representations of three-dimensional space?** Students may struggle with perceiving the depth in the images and interpreting different towers as in front or behind one another. Some students may struggle with the aerial views. Remind them how important struggle is for brain growth. You may want to prompt students to put their model on the floor and hover over it to understand the aerial view and compare their work to the puzzle. For students struggling with the side views, you may want to compare these to the architectural drawings and help students notice what they can and cannot see, and how their minds fill in the towers hidden behind. Then have them move back to the puzzle drawings and try to interpret these with the same thinking.

- **How are students recording their work?** For students who are considering how to record the various cities they built to match a puzzle, ask them what makes their cities different. The differences will likely center on how many cubes are in each tower and the positions of the towers. You might ask: How could you capture these differences? Which view(s) could help you show what makes them different? How could labels help? For students creating their own puzzles, guide them to use the view provided in the puzzles as models for how they might record their own cities. Ask, How did these views show the city? What views would help another person build your city? Students might also benefit from encouragement to focus on a single view and talk about what they see before they try to draw. Finally, you might also encourage students to go see how other partnerships are recording their thinking and learn from each other.

- **Are students seeing more than one way to construct the city?** Students might see the first way they construct as the only way the puzzle could work. Once they have built one way that they can prove matches the views they were given, encourage students to ask themselves, What could we change about this city and still have it match the views? Encourage students to try altering the city and checking it against the views to figure out what kinds of changes work.

Reflect

What is volume?

Architectural Drawing—Front and Side View

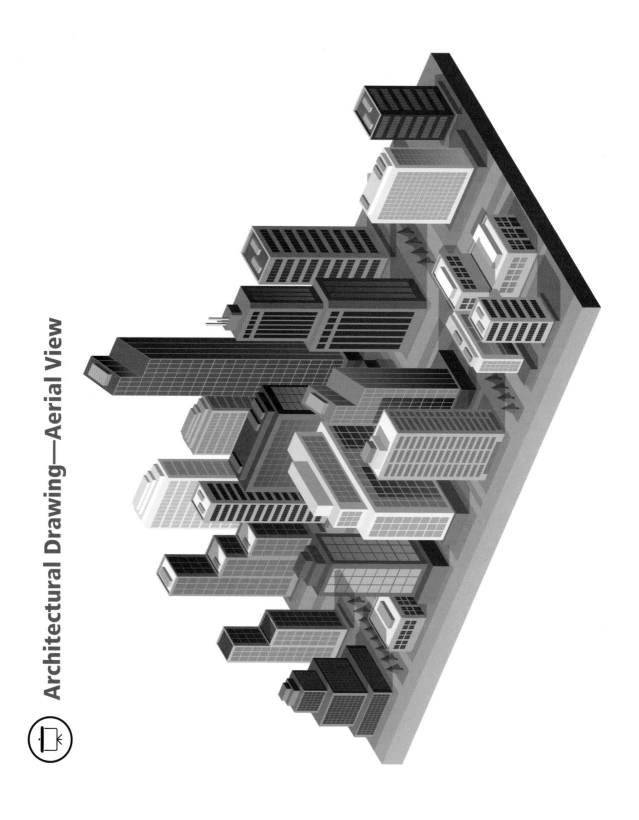

Architectural Drawing—Aerial View

City of Cubes Puzzle

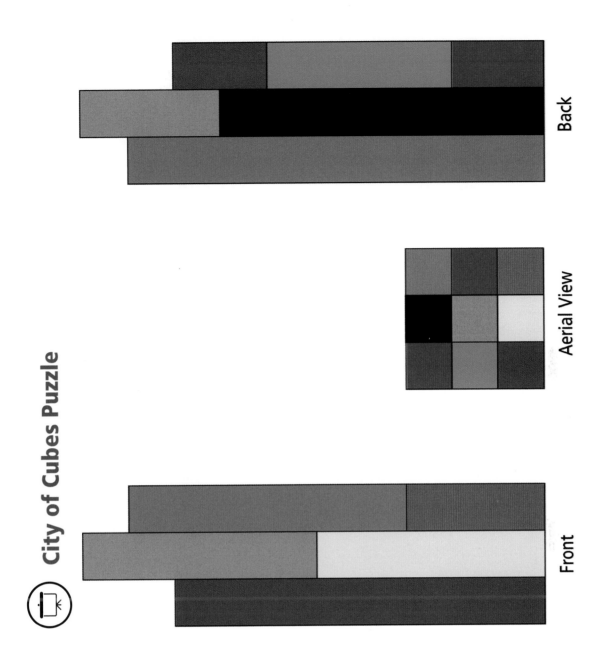

Back

Aerial View

Front

City of Cubes Puzzle

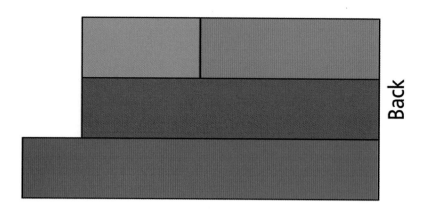

Back

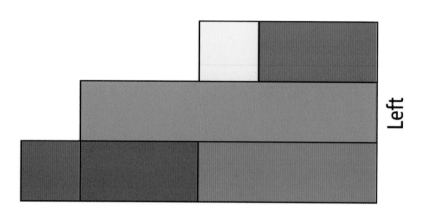

Left

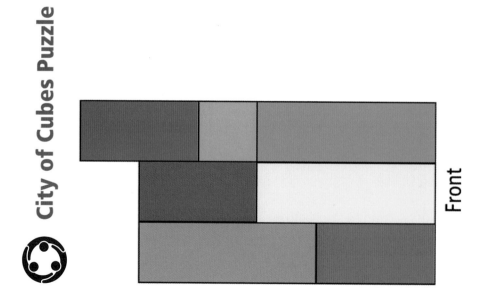

Front

City of Cubes Puzzle

Each color represents a building.
Builds of the same color are the same height.

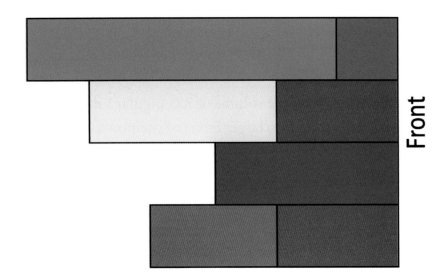

Front

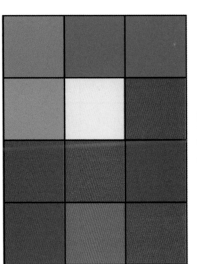

Aerial View

A Box of Boxes

Snapshot

Students investigate the volume of rectangular solids by packing little boxes into larger boxes of their own design, while trying to minimize the volume of empty space.

Connection to CCSS
5.MD.3
5.MD.4
5.MD.5

Agenda

Activity	Time	Description/Prompt	Materials
Launch	10 min	Show students some small boxes and discuss what happens when you pack them into a larger box to mail. Show students images of four small boxes and challenge them to design a box to hold them all.	• Examples of boxes for packing • Little Boxes sheet, to show class
Explore	30 min	Partners work to design boxes to hold a set of small boxes that they can construct from cubes: $3 \times 1 \times 1$, $2 \times 2 \times 2$, $3 \times 2 \times 2$, and $3 \times 2 \times 1$. Partners try to create a box with the smallest volume of empty space.	• Snap or multilink cubes, 30 per partnership • Little Boxes sheet, for each partnership • Isometric dot or grid paper (see appendix), for partners to record (See Play lesson) • Optional: colors
Discuss	15 min	Discuss the solutions students discovered and how to minimize empty space. Record students' solutions in a table to focus attention on dimensions and volume.	Chart and markers

Activity	Time	Description/Prompt	Materials
Explore	30+ min	Partners investigate minimizing empty space by changing the parameter of the problem. They can remove a little box, add a new little box, or create an entirely new set of little boxes. They try to design packing boxes for their sets that minimize empty space. Some students may investigate the opposite: what set of boxes requires a lot of empty space.	• Snap or multilink cubes, at least 30 per partnership • Little Boxes sheet, for each partnership • Box of Boxes Recording Sheet, at least one per partnership
Discuss	15+ min	Students share their findings from their various investigations, and the class discusses how thinking about volume helps in designing boxes.	Students' work

To the Teacher

The idea of packing boxes inside of a larger box may be familiar to some students, but it can be difficult to discuss with clarity. We encourage you to launch the lesson by showing some smaller boxes, and perhaps a larger packing box, so that students can clearly see the idea. You may want to ask students when they have seen this before—such as getting a package in the mail or packing a lunchbox—to help them make connections. You may want to show students what happens when a box is too large for its contents to help motivate them to create a box with the smallest volume of empty space.

The second half of the activity includes four avenues for investigation: removing a little box, adding a new little box, creating a set of boxes with no empty space, and creating a set of boxes that requires a lot of empty space. Given the range of choices, the class may find that this investigation stretches across multiple days. Students may want to spend one day exploring one of these questions and then try a new question the following day. The longer that students investigate, the more connections and patterns they will discover that support them in reasoning about volume and lead them toward multiplicative thinking.

Activity

Launch

Launch the investigation by showing the class a collection of boxes. You might use some boxes from around your classroom or school, such as boxes for tissues, paper clips, games, snacks, file folders, pencils, or markers. Make sure your collection includes boxes of different sizes. Ask students to imagine that you need to pack these different boxes into a larger box to send in the mail. When you mail a package, you want to make sure there is as little empty space as possible, to prevent the objects inside from rattling around, to conserve paper, and to protect the box from getting squashed. How would you choose the right size box? What is the smallest box you could fit all of these little boxes into?

Tell students that for today's investigation, they will be trying to find the smallest box that can hold a collection of smaller boxes. Show students the images of the four boxes they will be trying to fit together into a larger box: $3 \times 1 \times 1$, $2 \times 2 \times 2$, $3 \times 2 \times 2$, and $3 \times 2 \times 1$. Tell students that we name rectangular solids like these by their dimensions and that we say that a box measures "3 by 2 by 1" cubes. Point out these dimensions in the drawings and be sure students understand the language used.

The goal is for students to design a box that will hold all four and have the least amount of empty space when packed. The box must be a rectangular solid, as typical packing boxes are.

Explore

Provide students with snap or multilink cubes, a copy of the Little Boxes sheet, and isometric dot or grid paper (see appendix) to record their thinking. You may also want to provide colors for students to color-code the different little boxes in their drawings. Students work in partnerships to design a box that can hold the following smaller boxes: $3 \times 1 \times 1$, $2 \times 2 \times 2$, $3 \times 2 \times 2$, and $3 \times 2 \times 1$. The large box must be a rectangular solid. As students work, they should investigate the following questions:

- What is the smallest box you can make that will hold all of these boxes?
- What are the dimensions of your box? What is its volume? How much empty space will be left in your box?

Partners record their different solutions on isometric dot or grid paper (see appendix) as they try to find the smallest box with the least amount of empty space. For each solution, students record the dimensions of the packing box, the volume, and the empty space. This will help them compare their different solutions.

Discuss

When students have had a chance to investigate and come up with some possible solutions, gather them together to discuss the questions here. Record students' solutions on a chart showing the dimensions of each box, its volume, and the empty space remaining (Figure 1.3).

- What boxes did you create?
- How did you find the volume of the boxes you created?
- How did you figure out the amount of empty space in each of your packing boxes? What box leaves the least amount of empty space?

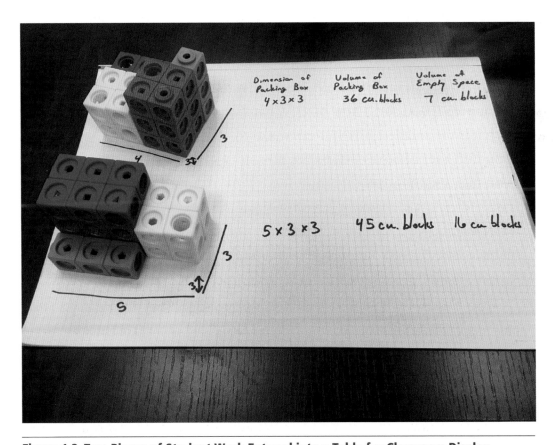

Figure 1.3 Two Pieces of Student Work Entered into a Table for Classroom Display

- What strategies did you come up with for minimizing the empty space?
- How can we be sure that we, as a class, have found the smallest packing box possible?

Ask students to look at the chart you have created out of the class's solutions. Ask, What patterns do you notice in the chart? Take advantage of connections students make between the dimensions of the packing box and its volume and the relationship between the packing box volume and the empty space volume (that is, the bigger the box, the more empty space it leaves).

Explore

After the discussion, challenge students to investigate what happens to the smallest packing box when they change the parameters of the problem. Students can choose to explore one or more of the following questions. For each question partners explore, they record the dimensions of the little boxes they are working with, the dimensions of the packing box, its volume, and the volume of empty space. A recording sheet is provided, though students may want to devise their own recording method.

- What happens if you remove one of the four small boxes? Now what is the smallest box you can make to hold the three remaining boxes?
- What happens if you add a new box? What size box would you want to add? Now what is the smallest box you can make to hold all five boxes?
- Can you find a set of boxes that leaves no empty space?
- Can you find a set of boxes that must leave a lot of empty space?

Discuss

Students will have investigated different constraints for packing boxes: packing fewer boxes, packing more boxes, packing with no empty space, and packing with lots of empty space. You'll want to discuss all of these pathways for investigation, but if one of them was more intriguing for students, be sure to give it extra time in your discussion. You may want to have students share their recording sheets on a document camera to show their solutions and how they refined their ideas through multiple trials.

- What interesting things did you discover when trying to pack boxes?
- What kinds of small boxes are challenging to pack? Why?

- What happens to the box you can make when you change what's inside?
- How did you refine your strategies for finding the smallest box?
- Did anyone find a set of boxes that leaves no empty space? Why does that work for these boxes?
- Did anyone find a set of boxes that you think must leave a lot of empty space? Why do you think this set requires a lot of empty space?
- How does thinking about volume help you design a packing box?

Look-Fors

- **Are students constructing an outer box of cubes around their little boxes?** Students might try to use the cubes to build a box around the smaller cubes, encasing them in additional cubes. This will create misleading solutions, because the cubes themselves have volume—they are actually little boxes. You may want to bring students back to the example cardboard boxes you shared in the launch to notice that packing boxes are thin. They might benefit from actually making the walls of the larger box out of paper (rather than cubes) to see that the box can be measured in cubes based on what is inside.

- **How are students finding the volume of empty space?** Some students may be able to imagine the missing cubes from the packing box they construct, but other students will need to see them. You might encourage students to fill in the missing space with a different color of cubes to help them see. They can then remove them to count the cubes representing empty space.

- **How are students finding the volume of the packing box?** Encourage students to build with cubes and count if that helps them. But you'll also want to push students to notice patterns that help them count faster and ultimately see volume as multiplicative. For instance, if students count the cubes on the bottom of their box (or in any layer), you might ask, Is there a way you could use that information so that you don't have to count all of the cubes? Pushing students to develop new ways will encourage brain growth.

Reflect

How do you find the volume of a rectangular solid?

Little Boxes

You have four shapes as shown below. What is the smallest size box that will fit these four shapes inside it?

The box must be a rectangular prism with length, width, and height. Is there more than one way to pack these shapes?

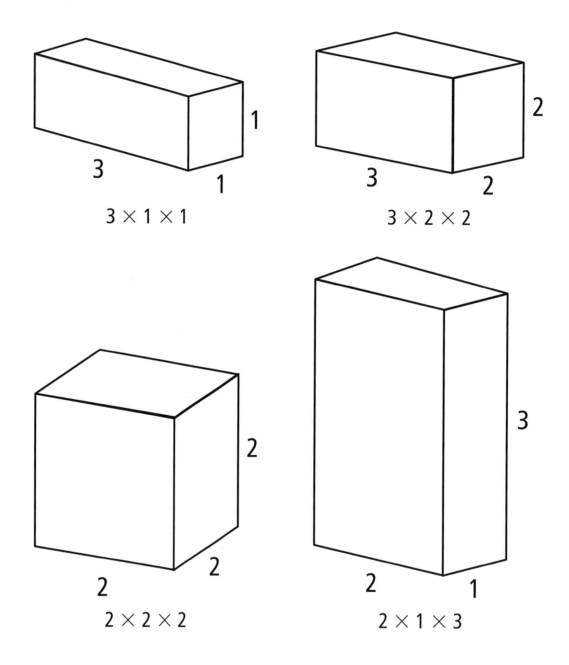

$3 \times 1 \times 1$

$3 \times 2 \times 2$

$2 \times 2 \times 2$

$2 \times 1 \times 3$

⬤ Box of Boxes Recording Sheet

Dimensions of Little Boxes	Dimensions of Packing Box	Volume of Packing Box	Volume of Empty Space

Estimating with Fractions

Many years ago in England, a government committee was commissioned to find out the mathematics most used by people in their lives and work. In 1982, *Mathematics Counts* was published, dubbed the "Cockcroft Report" after the chair of the committee—it was the first study of its kind. (www.educationengland.org.uk/documents/cockcroft/cockcroft1982.html#00). The panel highlighted a number of areas of mathematics that were used in people's jobs and lives. Many of them, such as arithmetic, were expected, and already take up a central role in mathematics teaching. But one area of mathematics the committee highlighted plays a minimal role in students' mathematical preparation. They addressed the vast importance of estimation, saying that industry and commerce rely "extensively" on the ability to estimate. The committee highlighted two aspects of estimation: first, being able and willing to judge whether the result of a calculation or measurement is reasonable; second, being able to make "subjective judgments" about measures—that is, giving a rough idea for a result, rather than working it out precisely. In my experience in many different classrooms over decades of work in mathematics education, I have found students to be unwilling, even afraid, to estimate results of calculations. Often when they are asked to estimate, students will work out the answer precisely and then round the numbers to make them seem like estimates! This reluctance to estimate often comes because students do not see estimating as being mathematical. They have spent so long calculating precisely, the idea of giving a rough estimate is alien to them. Yet this, it turns out, is critical to life and work.

Estimation is also a valuable activity because it helps with the development of number sense. If students are not calculating, they need to consider the approximate size of numbers or measures, and that will help develop critical areas of mathematics: number sense. In the set of three activities that make up this big idea, we ask students to estimate with fractions. This is ideal, as students often learn fractions as a set of procedures. When students are asked to estimate with fractions it helps them to move them away from the damaging idea that fractions are just a set of rules. Instead they will be asked to think more broadly about fraction sizes—about what they mean and how big they are, and how they relate to real objects. As with most of our activities, this will also encourage brain connections, as the mathematics is both numerical and visual.

In our Visualize activity, we invite students to make snowflakes, which will be engaging and will offer opportunities for deep thinking. As students work with their snowflakes, they will also think about fractions and sizes, estimating the fractions of papers they use. They will also be asked to think carefully about their estimates and whether they are close to the actual numbers, and how they would know.

In our Play activity, students will extend their work with snowflakes to develop strategies for cutting away specific fractions of paper, making a snowflake display for the room. The completed display creates a good discussion possibility wherein students can talk together about fraction estimation strategies and patterns. It is likely that as students work to cut away specific fractional parts, they will make mistakes— which gives you a wonderful opportunity to talk about the value of mistakes and to remind students that when they are struggling and finding things difficult, their brains are getting a really good workout with a lot of brain growth.

In our Investigate activity, students will use photographs to pose fraction estimation questions and will take their own photographs to create fraction estimation challenges. Students will be excited about being given the chance to take their own photographs of objects and to make their own mathematics questions. This is an important time for students to act with agency and to be creative, both of which are really critical in mathematics work.

Jo Boaler

Making Snowflakes

Snapshot

Students begin to think about estimating with fractions by making paper snowflakes and developing strategies for estimating the portion of paper they have cut away.

Connection to CCSS
5.NF.2

Agenda

Activity	Time	Description/Prompt	Materials
Launch	10 min	Show students how you might cut out a snowflake from a piece of square paper. Discuss as a class the question, About how much of the paper has been cut away? Introduce the idea of estimating with fractions.	• Sheet of square white paper • Scissors • Sheet of colored paper
Explore	30+ min	Partners cut out their own paper snowflakes and develop ways to estimate the portion of paper that has been cut away for each.	• Square paper, multiple sheets per partnership • Scissors, one per partnership • Colored construction paper, multiple sheets per partnership • Tape • Chart paper and markers
Discuss	15 min	Discuss the strategies students developed for estimating the fraction of paper missing from their snowflakes. Discuss the challenges of estimating with fractions and what students might do to increase their precision.	Students' charts

To the Teacher

We've called this activity Making Snowflakes because many students will have had prior experience with folding paper, cutting out portions, and opening the paper up to discover what they've made. These figures do not need to be snowflakes, and some students might be more interested in simply creating patterns. Folding and cutting produces repetition, which can be used to estimate the portion of paper cut away, and we encourage you to make this a central part of the task, regardless of what students make.

Some students may struggle with the notion that we can estimate with fractions. When students typically work with fractions, precision is often emphasized. We want to make sure that each portion is exactly equal, and we use this precision to compare close fractions, such as $\frac{2}{3}$ and $\frac{3}{4}$. But fractions are numbers and can be used to estimate, which deepens students' understanding of these values. In this lesson, encourage students to use benchmark fractions to reason about the fraction of paper they have cut away, and to use their knowledge of comparing fractions to identify fractions between benchmarks. If students say that their estimate is between $\frac{1}{4}$ and $\frac{1}{2}$, you might ask them whether they think it is closer to $\frac{1}{4}$ or $\frac{1}{2}$, and then what fraction it might be. Estimating encourages us to reason because an exact answer is not possible; all answers require a clear justification.

Activity

Launch

Launch the lesson by showing students how you might fold paper to make a snow-flake. Fold a square piece of paper into equal-size pieces radiating from a central point. You could fold it into sixths as snowflakes actually are, but eighths are fine, too. Then cut some portions out. Hold up the paper before you unfold it, and ask students to look at what you've cut away and the paper that is still in your hand. Then unfold the paper and tape it to a colored piece of paper to make the holes more visible, as shown in Figure 2.1.

Ask students, About how much of the paper did I cut away? Have them turn and talk to a partner about their estimate. Ask students to share some thoughts with the class about this question. Highlight ideas that use fractions to consider the portion that has been cut away. If students do not use fractions at all, but instead use descriptive language (for example, "some" or "a little bit"), push them to think about how they could make their description more precise. Students may say something like, "less than half," and you might ask students what fraction it could be if it is less than one half.

Ask students, Why are fractions a useful way of talking about how much paper I cut away? Discuss briefly how fractions let us name the part of the whole, comparing the part removed from the piece of paper we started with. Make explicit that

a. A red snowflake pattern glued to a yellow background piece.

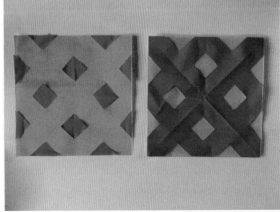

b. A blue snowflake glued to a sheet of orange paper. The remaining blue squares are glued to another sheet of orange paper.

Figure 2.1

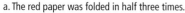

the fraction(s) students came up with are estimates, not measurements, and that in today's work we are going to explore how we can estimate with fractions. Introduce students to the task and make your own snowflake available if students want to look at how it was created.

Explore

Students should have access to square paper, colored construction paper, scissors, and tape. Ask students to work with a partner to fold a square piece of paper and cut out portions to create a paper snowflake, as shown in Figure 2.2. These paper cutouts may look like snowflakes, but they certainly don't need to. Any cutout creation will work for this exploration. Students may want to tape their snowflakes to colored construction paper, as you did, to make it easier to see the missing portion.

For each snowflake students make, they should come up with a way to estimate the fraction of the paper they have cut away. Ask students to make a display on chart paper showing their snowflakes and how they estimated the fraction of missing paper. They may want to annotate the snowflake or the cut-away portions to help make their process or argument clear, as shown in Figure 2.3.

If there is time, ask students to make multiple snowflakes and see whether their strategies for estimating are effective for different snowflakes or whether they need new methods.

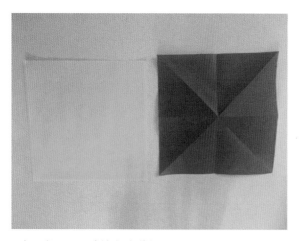 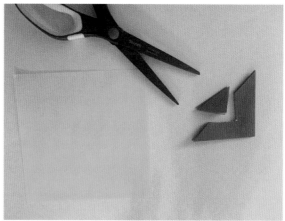

a. The red paper was folded in half three times.

b. One cut was made from the folded red paper.

Figure 2.2

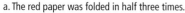

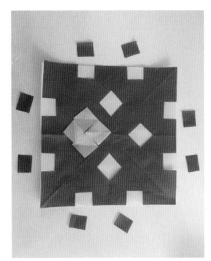
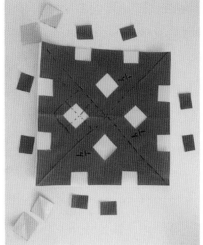

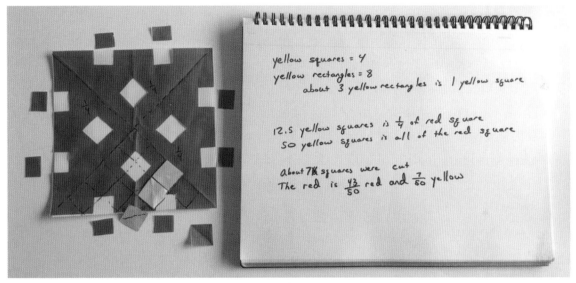

yellow squares = 4
yellow rectangles = 8
    about 3 yellow rectangles is 1 yellow square

12.5 yellow squares is $\frac{1}{4}$ of red square
50 yellow squares is all of the red square

about 7½ squares were cut
The red is $\frac{43}{50}$ red and $\frac{7}{50}$ yellow

Figure 2.3 The Progression of Work That Results in an Estimate

Discuss

Have students post their charts where the class can see them. Discuss the following questions, referring to students' work whenever possible:

- What strategies did you come up with for estimating the fraction of paper that was missing?
- What did you use to help you? (Encourage students to think about what ideas or patterns they used to help them estimate. Some may use the holes in the snowflake; others might use the cut-away bits to think about the fraction of paper that is missing.)

- What was hard about making an estimate?
- How close do you think your estimates are? Why? Do you think your estimates are over or under the actual fraction that is missing?
- How could you check your estimate or make it more precise?

Look-Fors

- **How are students getting started with their estimates?** Students might cut out a snowflake and simply not know how to begin estimating. It may be helpful to make all the components of the problem visible by laying out the snowflake, the cut-out parts, and an uncut sheet of paper. You could ask students how they might use these to help them think about the part that has been cut away. You might ask students to start describing it with words, such as "some," "a little," or "most," and then connect those words to the benchmark fraction $\frac{1}{2}$ by asking, "When you say 'some,' is that more or less than $\frac{1}{2}$?" Once students have an entry point, you might ask them to think about how close to $\frac{1}{2}$ it is or what other benchmarks they could use to help them get closer to an estimate.

- **Are students trying to be exact, instead of estimating?** Some students might engage in measurement or strategic cutting to try to find an exact answer. Encourage students to take the risk to be less precise because the goal is to develop ways of estimating with fractions. For students who try to make lots of measurements or to calculate area, you may want to point out that, although precise, these are time-consuming methods when an estimate is all that is needed.

- **How are students using benchmark fractions to estimate?** Some students might categorize all snowflakes as having $\frac{1}{4}$, $\frac{1}{2}$, or $\frac{3}{4}$ of the paper cut away. Support students in thinking in more nuanced ways by asking them to reason about the missing paper's relationship to the benchmark. Is it more or less than the benchmark? A little or a lot more/less? What fraction values are in that neighborhood? These questions can help students develop better estimates and reason about fractions in relationship to one another.

Reflect

What do you think was the most effective (or interesting) strategy for estimating the fraction of paper that was cut away? Why?

Fraction Blizzard

Snapshot

Students extend their work with snowflakes to develop strategies for cutting away a specific fraction of the paper: $\frac{1}{8}$, $\frac{1}{6}$, $\frac{1}{4}$, $\frac{1}{3}$, $\frac{1}{2}$, or $\frac{3}{4}$. The class creates a snowflake display they can use to discuss fraction estimation strategies and patterns.

Connection to CCSS
5.NF.2

Agenda

Activity	Time	Description/Prompt	Materials
Launch	10 min	Remind students of the strategies they developed for estimating the fraction of paper cut away from their snowflakes in the Visualize activity. Challenge students to create snowflakes that target particular fractions.	• Charts or examples of student work from the Visualize activity • Display area set up with labels for the different snowflakes
Play	30+ min	Partners work together to create snowflakes that have $\frac{1}{8}$, $\frac{1}{6}$, $\frac{1}{4}$, $\frac{1}{3}$, $\frac{1}{2}$, or $\frac{3}{4}$ of the paper cut away. They develop strategies for targeting particular fractions and refine their strategies for estimating. Students post their snowflakes on a class display.	• Square paper, multiple sheets per partnership • Scissors, one per partnership • Construction paper, multiple sheets per partnership • Tape or glue • Tools for posting the snowflakes: tape, pushpins, or stapler

(Continued)

Activity	Time	Description/Prompt	Materials
Discuss	15–20 min	Discuss the strategies students developed for targeting a specific fraction and any patterns they noticed as they worked. Use the class display to determine whether the snowflakes make sense, and discuss any that don't seem to fit.	Students' work on the class display
Extend	20+ min	Partners choose their own challenging fraction to target (for instance, $\frac{3}{8}$, $\frac{1}{7}$, or $\frac{5}{6}$) and test the strategies they have developed on these fractions.	• Square paper, multiple sheets per partnership • Scissors, one per partnership • Construction paper, multiple sheets per partnership • Tape or glue

To the Teacher

Just as in the Visualize activity, we have framed this lesson as creating snowflakes, but students can create any kind of cut-out pattern by folding and cutting paper. The use of folding with cutting creates repetition, which is useful for estimating the fraction of paper that will be cut away.

Before the lesson, we encourage you to set up a display area for the snowflakes students create. You might use a wall, bulletin board, or whiteboard. Label an area for each target fraction of paper cut away: $\frac{1}{8}$, $\frac{1}{6}$, $\frac{1}{4}$, $\frac{1}{3}$, $\frac{1}{2}$, and $\frac{3}{4}$ of the paper missing. Students will use this space to post the snowflakes for each target fraction, so make sure the space is large enough to accommodate the number of snowflakes your class will create. See Figure 2.4 for an example.

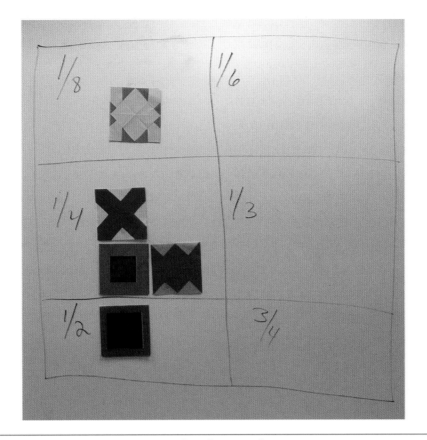

Figure 2.4 Five pieces of student work are already posted!

Activity

Launch

Launch the lesson by reminding students of the work they did in the Visualize activity to cut out snowflakes and estimate the fraction of the paper they cut away. You may want to refer to students' posters and name some of the strategies they developed, because these strategies will likely be useful in today's work. Tell students that today they will be trying to create snowflakes with different fractions of paper cut away. Show students the display area and the labels you have created for their snowflakes. Ask, How could you create a snowflake that cuts away about $\frac{1}{8}$ of the paper? How could you create a snowflake that cuts away about $\frac{1}{6}$ of the paper? $\frac{1}{4}$? $\frac{1}{3}$? $\frac{1}{2}$? Can you create a snowflake that cuts away about $\frac{3}{4}$ of the paper? Remind students that they are still estimating—not measuring—but that their strategies and reasoning matter. Partners work together to come up with ways to target a specific fraction and justify their reasoning.

Play

Provide students with square paper, construction paper, scissors, and tools for posting their snowflakes on the wall. Students work in partners to develop methods for creating snowflakes with about $\frac{1}{8}$, $\frac{1}{6}$, $\frac{1}{4}$, $\frac{1}{3}$, $\frac{1}{2}$, and $\frac{3}{4}$ of the paper removed.

Partners first choose a fraction of paper they will try to cut away. They will likely need to try several different times, and will need access to lots of paper. Encourage this experimentation and students' willingness to make mistakes in trying to solve these puzzles. When partners think their snowflake matches the chosen fraction, ask them to mount it on a piece of construction paper. Then partners should show how they made their estimate of paper removed. Students might diagram the snowflake and use labels, arrows, words, and numbers to show their evidence for the approximate fraction of paper cut away. Then students post their snowflake with written evidence on the class display under the fraction label that matches their target fraction.

Encourage students to try several fractions as they develop methods for getting close to a target fraction.

Discuss

Once students have had a chance to make several snowflakes, make lots of mistakes, and revise, bring them together to discuss the following questions. Be sure to refer to the snowflakes on the display whenever possible.

- What strategies did you come up with for making a snowflake with a target fraction of paper removed?
- What did you use to help you? (Encourage kids to think about what ideas or patterns they used to help them estimate.)
- Which fractions were harder or easier? Why?
- What was hard about targeting an estimate?
- Looking at the wall, do the snowflakes under each fraction make sense? For example, do all the snowflakes under $\frac{1}{2}$ look like they have about the same amount of paper removed? (If the class notices any that seem different, you may want to talk about them as a class.)
- Are there other fractions you would like to try? What might make other fractions interesting or challenging?

Extend

If students are engaged in snowflake making and want to try more, you could ask them to select their own target fractions and create new snowflakes to match. You might encourage them to select fractions they think will be challenging in some way, perhaps because they are not unit fractions (such as $\frac{3}{8}$), are large (such as $\frac{5}{6}$), or are less friendly (such as $\frac{1}{7}$). This will encourage students to build their estimation capacities to include a broader group of fractions.

Look-Fors

- **Are students cutting strategically?** Although we encourage students to make lots of mistakes, students will learn the most from their mistakes if they are working strategically. If students appear to be working at random, you might ask them to tell you about their plan or what they are trying. You could also have them look back at their earlier attempts and reflect on why those didn't meet their target fraction. Did they cut away too much or not enough paper? How could they adjust what they did in a previous snowflake to get closer to their goal?
- **How are students estimating?** Estimating the fraction of paper removed can be challenging, and you may encounter students who create snowflakes and are struggling to determine whether they match their target fraction. Revisit strategies used in the Visualize activity and ask students which of those strategies makes the most sense to them. Support students in trying out their strategies with a snowflake they have already made.

- **How are students explaining their estimates?** Students might have an estimate that was developed intentionally, but struggle to explain their process. Often it helps to use the snowflake itself or the cut-out pieces to support them in explaining their reasoning. Ask students to show you how they are thinking about the estimate, to help you visualize what they can see in their own minds. If students are stuck, you can also ask them to name or write down what they know about their snowflake and then bring this to the class in the discussion so that other students can help construct an explanation.

Reflect

What makes a fraction easier or harder to estimate?

Wondering with Fractions
Snapshot

Students pose fraction estimation questions using photographs of collections and aerial images. Partners investigate their questions and develop strategies for fraction estimation.

Connection to CCSS
5.NF.2

Agenda

Activity	Time	Description/Prompt	Materials
Launch	10 min	Remind students of their earlier work with fraction estimation with snowflakes. Show students one of the fraction estimation photos and ask students to generate their own questions that they are curious about. Encourage them to ask questions that involve fraction estimation.	• One Fraction Estimation Image sheet to show the class • Chart and markers
Explore	30+ min	Partners choose a photo and generate fraction estimation questions. Then partners develop strategies for answering their questions, recording their methods on charts to share.	• Fraction Estimation Image sheets, multiple copies of each sheet per partnership • Tape • Charts and marker, for each partnership
Discuss	15 min	Do a gallery walk of students' charted photos, questions, and strategies for fraction estimation. Discuss the questions and strategies students developed, and the connections between them.	• Partners' charts posted around the room • Dot stickers in two colors, a few per student

(Continued)

Activity	Time	Description/Prompt	Materials
Extend	45+ min	Partners construct their own fraction estimation photos. Then they pose and solve fraction estimation questions about their pictures. Partners can then swap photos with other groups to explore.	• Tablets or cameras for taking photos • Access to objects around the classroom for staging photos • Ways to view photos: tablets, computers, or printouts

To the Teacher

In students' previous work with snowflakes, they were reasoning about area when estimating the fraction of paper cut away. Area is a useful place to start when learning to estimate with fractions, because when a part looks bigger, it is also a bigger fraction of the whole. However, there are many situations involving estimating with fractions where the parts are not of equal size, and being larger may not be relevant. In fact, being larger can be misleading. In this lesson, we ask students to ask their own fraction questions using photographs as inspiration. Students will naturally ask fraction questions that involve both area and quantity. For instance, they may ask, What fraction of the beach has litter? This question is asking about the fraction of the area of the beach. They might also ask, What fraction of the buttons are blue? This question is asking about the fraction of the quantity of buttons. The difference between estimating as part of a whole and estimating as part of a set will make for a great discussion.

In the extension, students can create their own photos to use for fraction estimation. Students will be excited about this challenge, and we encourage you to give students access to a variety of objects, supplies, materials, and places with which to design and take their photos. Students might use collections you already have, such as a jumbled bin of markers, or create orderly arrays of objects. Students may need to create these displays on the floor so that they can stand over them to get the best aerial shots of their arrangements. Alternatively, students may want to take advantage of natural displays, such as books in the library, supplies ordered in a closet, collections of sports equipment, or students in the cafeteria. The key element is that partners are intrigued by the image they capture and want to use it to pose and answer their own fraction estimation question. We see this as part of developing the disposition to see the world—and to wonder—mathematically.

Activity

Launch

Launch the lesson by reminding students of the work they have done with estimating the fraction of paper removed from their snowflakes. Tell students that today we're going to estimate with fractions in a different way, starting by asking some fraction estimation questions.

Show students one of the fraction estimation photos, such as those shown in Figure 2.5. Ask them to turn and talk to a partner about what they notice in the photo. For this turn and talk, you just want students to make sense of the complex image and notice some of the parts. Ask students to share what they've noticed.

Then ask students what fraction estimation questions they could pose of this picture. You may want to tell students that fraction estimation questions might sound like, "About what fraction . . .?" Give students another opportunity to turn and talk to a partner to generate some questions. Ask students to share questions about the picture, and record students' ideas on a chart.

Tell students that they will be generating their own fraction questions, like these, and working to develop strategies for estimating the answers. Remind students that precision is not needed here, just a reasoned estimate.

Explore

Make available copies of the Fraction Estimation Image sheets, tape, charts, and markers. Partners choose a photo they would like to start with and use it to generate some fraction estimation questions that they might ask of the picture. Some students may want to start with the photo you shared with the class, and the class's questions.

Source: Shutterstock.com/Viktor Gladkov

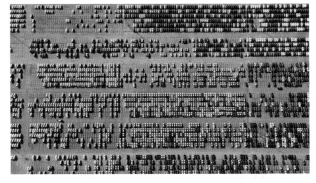

Source: Shutterstock.com/wponpai

Figure 2.5 Fraction Estimation Images

Then partners work together to develop strategies for answering some of their questions. Students should be sure to document their process on a chart. They may want to attach the photo to the chart, and record their questions, too. Partners should be ready to explain and justify their methods.

Students may want to explore multiple photos, generating new questions for each. Partners can try the methods they have developed on these photos, and develop new methods, too. For each photo students explore, they should create a new chart to document their questions and solutions.

Discuss

Have partners post their charts around the classroom. You may want to group together those charts that explore the same photo. Give students dot stickers in two colors, such as yellow and blue. Ask partners to do a gallery walk around the classroom to examine the posters everyone created. While they walk, students use their two colors of dots to mark (1) the most interesting questions groups asked and (2) methods they would like to discuss or see explained.

Gather students together to discuss the results of the gallery walk and their reflections on their own work. Discuss the following:

- What interesting fraction estimation questions did groups ask? (You may want to point out the questions that students placed their dots near and ask why they found these questions to be interesting. Celebrate the range of questions students posed.)
- What strategies did you invent? What strategies would you like to hear more about? (Students may want to share their own strategies, or you may want to use the dot vote to select specific strategies for students to share.)
- What connections do you notice between the different strategies that we used?
- Did you find yourself using different strategies for different questions? When were different strategies useful?
- How were these strategies similar to or different from the strategies we used with snowflakes?

Extend

Partners work together to create their own fraction estimation photos using things in their classroom or school environment. You may want to ask students to look back at the photos provided in this lesson and notice what made them good images for fraction estimation. For instance, these images contain a lot of individual objects or living things, too many to reasonably count. The images also include some variation across those individual things, such as different colors, shapes, sizes, quantities, or types. The kinds of features make the photos particularly well suited for asking fraction estimation questions.

Provide partners with a camera or tablet. Challenge students to design, stage, and capture a photo about which they would be interested in asking fraction estimation questions. Give students access to materials around the classroom, such as manipulatives, books, and office supplies, with which they might construct interesting photos. Students may want to take photos around the school, such as of rows of books on the library shelves or tiles in the hallway. Encourage creativity and variety. Make sure students are excited about the images they create.

Once partners have captured their photo, they will need a way to view it at a reasonable size. This could be on a tablet or computer screen or printed out on paper. Ask students to generate questions about their photo and try to answer them. You may want to make students' photos available to other partnerships to explore, asking and trying to answer their own question.

You may want to discuss with students after this extension what the most interesting photos and questions were, and how they went about solving them.

Look-Fors

- **Are students estimating quantity or size?** After the snowflake activities, students will have lots of experience estimating by thinking about area or size. Some of the questions students may ask about these pictures will focus on area (such as, What fraction of the space in the photo is taken up by an object), and some will focus on quantity (such as, What fraction of the objects have a particular property). Estimating with area and estimating with quantity involve different ways of thinking and necessitate different strategies. Students may make area-based assumptions about quantity, such as assuming that there are the same number of large objects and small objects because half the space is taken up by each.

- **How are students estimating?** Students may estimate by thinking across the entire image or by using a portion of the image. For images that are uniform, sampling makes a lot of sense. It would be easier to find a fraction of a corner of the image and assume that this fraction applied across the whole picture. But if the image is not uniform, students will need to develop other ways of accounting for variation.

Reflect

What fraction questions are you wondering about now? What kinds of questions would you want to investigate if you could ask questions outside your school?

Fraction Estimation Image

Mindset Mathematics, Grade 5, copyright © 2018 by Jo Boaler, Jen Munson, Cathy Williams. Reproduced by permission of John Wiley & Sons, Inc. *Source:* Shutterstock.com/Viktor Gladkov

Fraction Estimation Image

Fraction Estimation Image

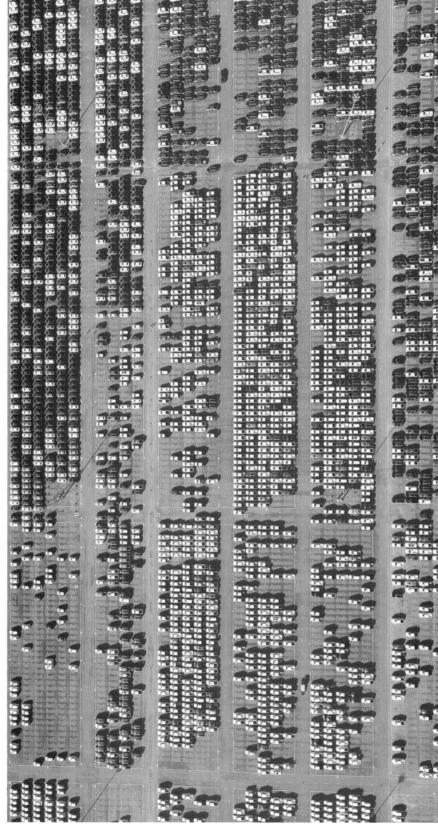

Fraction Estimation Image

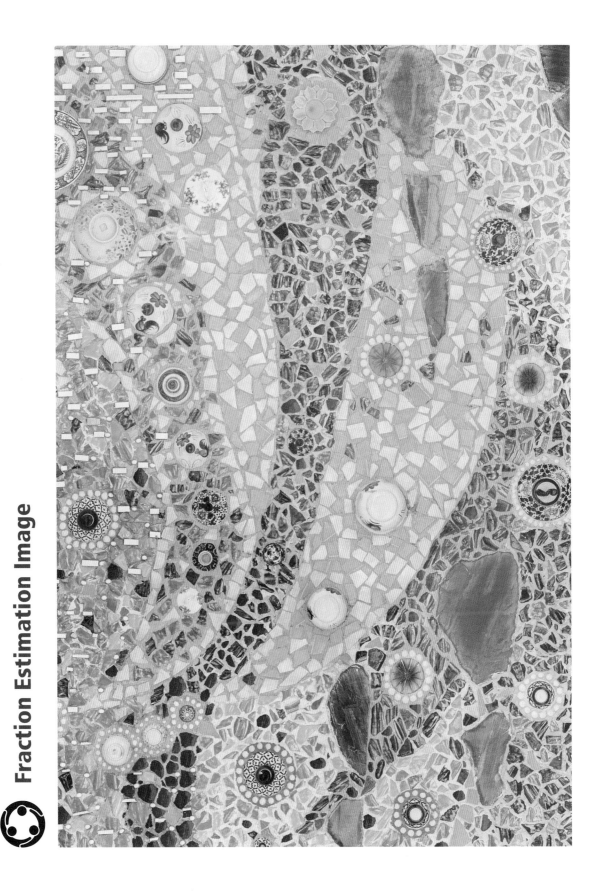

Fraction Estimation Image

Fraction Estimation Image

BIG IDEA 3

Using Fraction Equivalence

Fraction equivalence is at the heart of any work with fractions. Once students know how to make fractions equivalent, they can add them and subtract them, multiply and divide them more easily. More important perhaps, when students work to make fractions equivalent, they are working with the main idea inside fractions: that of a relationship. Students often become very confused by fractions, which is not surprising, as there are different rules for adding, subtracting, multiplying, and dividing. A common error that students often make when adding fractions is to add the numerator and the denominator: $\frac{1}{7} + \frac{2}{7} = \frac{3}{14}$, for example. Students are prone to making errors like this when they have learned fractions as a set of rules instead of as big ideas. One of the most important ideas that students need to understand when they meet fractions is that a fraction represents one number, not two, and that the single number comes from a relationship between the numerator and the denominator. We never know whether a fraction is big or small from the size of the numerator; we have to know how the numerator relates to the denominator. A fraction with 50 as a numerator is small if the denominator is 1,000 $\left(\frac{50}{1,000}\right)$, but large if the denominator is 60 $\left(\frac{50}{60}\right)$. Students have often learned to deal with fractions as though they are two separate numbers, so it makes sense to add $\frac{1}{7}$ to $\frac{2}{7}$ and get $\frac{3}{14}$. But if they are thinking about $\frac{1}{7}$ as a relationship and $\frac{2}{7}$ as a relationship, they may notice that together the two fractions are almost one half and nowhere near $\frac{3}{14}$. This is why the idea of a relationship is so key to fraction understanding yet often missed in the teaching of fractions.

When students are thinking about fractions as a relationship, they can more easily think about fraction equivalence, which is the big idea encapsulated in this set of activities. In the Visualize activity, we give students a set of paintings and accompanying puzzles. Similar questions could be used with other paintings and diagrams. The main idea of the activity is to give students an intuitive experience of thinking about denominators and to see some of the many connections between mathematics and art.

In the Play activity, students take on a detective role, looking for patterns in different paintings, exploring which ones might be genuine and which ones fakes by considering fractional representations. This gives students an interesting (we hope!) reason to use their developing understanding of fractions. Encourage students to be flexible in their use of fractions and to always value the times when they are struggling and making mistakes, as those are the most important times for their brain development.

In the Investigate activity, students are given the open question of dividing squares into different colored areas to show fraction differences. It is really good if they are encouraged to try many different ways of finding solutions. This helps give students the knowledge that any mathematics question can be solved with different methods and that this is part of the beauty of mathematics. Students are also using color, which helps makes mathematical ideas visual and interesting. We encourage you to make a class display of the solutions, as it should be very interesting and colorful, and is a good vehicle for revisiting the ideas over the school year.

Jo Boaler

Picking Paintings Apart

Snapshot

Exploring the colors used in geometric art, students build on their understanding of fraction equivalence to visualize the need for common denominators when adding and subtracting fractions.

Connection to CCSS
5.NF.1
5.NF.2

Agenda

Activity	Time	Description/Prompt	Materials
Launch	10 min	Introduce students to geometric artwork and some paintings that we've created, inspired by artists' work.	• Examples of geometric art from books or online • Three inspired paintings: Stacks, Nests, and Patches
Explore	20–30 min	Partners develop ways of finding the fraction of the area of a painting covered by two or more colors.	Stacks, Nests, and Patches handouts, one each per partnership
Discuss	15 min	Discuss the methods students developed for joining the fractions represented by the different colors. Name the reason for using the same size pieces (a common denominator) when joining.	Chart and markers

To the Teacher

This lesson begins with looking at examples of geometric artwork that you might find on museum websites or in art books in your school's library. You can find compelling examples among the works of Piet Mondrian, Frank Stella, and Ellsworth Kelly, whose work has inspired the images in this lesson. If your students have never seen this kind of artwork, you may want to spend some additional time looking at examples and talking about what students notice about the use of shapes, colors, and lines. It is worth the time to encourage students to notice the work mathematically and make connections between art and math.

The central mathematical idea in this lesson is the need to use units of the same size when joining two groups. In the case of fractions, the unit is the unit fraction or denominator. Students will use the paintings as places to decide what the unit size is and to explore why having units of the same size for the different colors is important for joining them together. Some students may join the colors together first and then determine a unit; others may think about each color separately and then try to join them. In either case, students will discover that finding a shared unit is critical for adding fractions. Students may not have language to name what it is that they are doing—indeed, "finding a common denominator" sounds like a mechanical endeavor. This activity is designed to give students an intuitive experience that they can draw on to understand that "finding a common denominator" is really about finding a unit size that can be used to build both fractions, something they can literally see in the paintings. Naming this concept mathematically is something we encourage you to do in the discussion, after students have seen the need to use equal-size pieces.

Activity

Launch

Launch the lesson by introducing students to some examples of geometric painting, such as the work of Mondrian, Stella, or Kelly. These artists use shape and color to express different feelings and create balance. Tell students that in today's activity, we're going to look at some examples of paintings that were inspired by these artists. Show students the three paintings for this task: Stacks, Nests, and Patches. For each of these paintings, we want to figure out what fraction of the painting is taken up by two or more of the colors together. Tell students that on the handouts, each painting has a question written underneath it. Read each of the questions to students and be sure they understand that they are looking for the fraction of the painting that is taken up by the two (or three) colors together. If you are working with the grayscale images, the questions have been adapted.

Explore

Students work in partners and choose a painting to start with. Each painting has its own puzzle:

- For Stacks: What fraction of the painting is yellow and orange together?
- For Nests: What fraction of the painting is purple and green together?
- For Patches: What fraction of the painting is color (red, blue, and yellow together)?

Provide students with copies of the painting they choose. Students should record their thinking so that they can share and justify their answers. Encourage students to use number sentences to label the work they have done. Encourage partners to solve as many of the puzzles as they can and to think about multiple ways to explain the answers they come up with so that the class will be convinced of their findings.

Discuss

Gather students together, along with their written work, and discuss the questions here. Be sure to record students' strategies on a chart or on the paintings themselves using a document camera. Having a shared record of the strategies and how we can label them with fractions will be useful for future work.

- How did you approach solving these problems? What strategies did you develop?
- How did you name the fraction for each color so you could join them? How did equivalent fractions help you?
- How did you label your work with number sentences? Are there any other number sentences that could be used to represent your strategy?
- What did you have to do in order to solve these problems?

In this discussion, be sure that the idea of using a common denominator or making the pieces the same size becomes clear. Labeling students' work with fractions, equivalent fractions, and number sentences serves to formalize this idea. If students have not labeled their own work, be sure to ask the class how it could be labeled.

Look-Fors

- **How are students labeling their work?** Students may subdivide the paintings and count pieces, then label their final answer, without writing a number sentence to label what they have done. Encourage students to return to their work and come up with a number sentence that could accurately represent what they did to join the two colors. Some students may think of these as subtraction problems—taking away the area of the other colors from the whole—while others may think of them as joining the colors together. In either case, a number sentence will help students name what they have done and formalize the relationships between different fractions they were using.
- **How are students dealing with fractions with different denominators?** Students may name the fractions involved in the task using different denominators and then not know how to proceed. For instance, in the Nests painting, some students might observe that the two squares that contain the green and purple represent $\frac{1}{2}$ of the painting, and all they need to do is subtract the two red squares, which are each $\frac{1}{100}$. With these different denominators, this useful observation would leave students stuck. Encourage students to go back to the painting and think about ways they could use the image to help them. For instance, in the Nests example, you might ask, How can you take these

little red pieces away from this larger part of the painting? If you know that each red is $\frac{1}{100}$, how can you use that to help you figure out what is left? Or what the green and purple are? Are there other fraction names you could use for these parts that would help you subtract?

Reflect

Why does the denominator matter when adding or subtracting fractions?

 **Stacks**

Inspired by *Red, Yellow, Blue,* by Ellsworth Kelly, 1963.

What fraction of the painting is yellow and orange?

Mindset Mathematics, Grade 5, copyright © 2018 by Jo Boaler, Jen Munson, Cathy Williams.
Reproduced by permission of John Wiley & Sons, Inc.

 **Stacks**

Inspired *Red, Yellow, Blue,* by Ellsworth Kelly, 1963.

What fraction of the painting is white (1) and light gray (2)?

Inspired by *Double Concentric: Scramble,* by Frank Stella, 1971.

What fraction of the painting is purple and green?

 **Nests**

Inspired by *Double Concentric: Scramble,* by Frank Stella, 1971.

What fraction of the painting is white (1) and dark gray (2)?

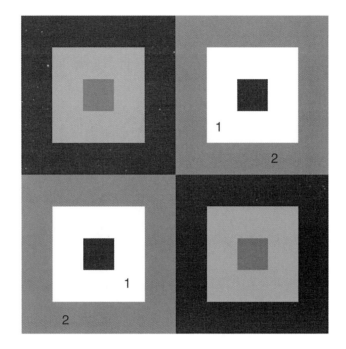

Inspired by *Composition II in Red, Blue, and Yellow,* by Piet Mondrian, 1921.

What fraction of the painting is red, blue, and yellow?

 **Patches**

Inspired by *Composition II in Red, Blue, and Yellow,* by Piet Mondrian, 1921.

What fraction of the painting is dark gray (1), medium gray (2), and light gray (3)?

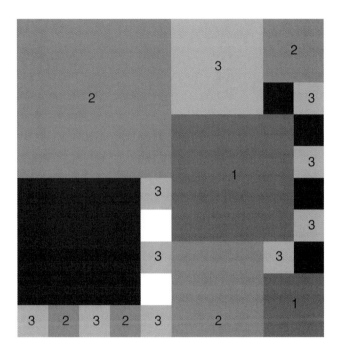

Make a Fake

Snapshot

Building on students' work with adding and subtracting fractions in geometric art, students create "good" and "close" fake Mondrian paintings. The class does detective work to find the close fakes, which are more than $\frac{1}{2}$ color.

Connection to CCSS
5.NF.1
5.NF.2

Agenda

Activity	Time	Description/Prompt	Materials
Launch	10 min	Show students some examples of Mondrian's geometric paintings from the 1940s and ask students to consider how they are similar to and different from Patches, a fake Mondrian used in the Visualize activity. Challenge students to make a better fake.	• Examples of Mondrian's paintings from books or online • Patches handout
Explore	30 min	Partners work together to either modify Patches or create their own fake so that it includes white, black, red, yellow, and blue, and so that color makes up no more than $\frac{1}{2}$ of the painting—a "good fake." Students also work to create a "close fake"—a painting with a little more than $\frac{1}{2}$ color. Students analyze their paintings.	• Patches handout, one per partnership • Dot paper (see appendix), multiple sheets per partnership • Colors • Analyzing Our Fake sheet, two per partnership
Discuss	20+ min	In a gallery walk, students do detective work on the paintings the class has created, trying to find the "good" and "close" fakes. Discuss their findings and what they had to consider in constructing their fakes.	• Students' paintings posted around the room • Optional: sticky notes

To the Teacher

At the heart of this lesson are the geometric paintings of Piet Mondrian, particularly those using rectangular regions of white, black, red, yellow, and blue. We encourage you to find some examples of these paintings to share with students at the start of this lesson, either on museum websites or in art books from your school's library. We suggest works from the 1940s such as *Broadway Boogie-Woogie* (1942), *Composition London* (1940–42), *New York City I* (1942), and *Composition No. 10* (1942).

The challenging mathematical work in this activity is in justifying why the three colors together are less than or a little more than $\frac{1}{2}$ of the painting. Push students to build on their understanding of the underlying grid provided by the dot paper (see appendix), then to name the fraction each color represents and how those fractions combine to something more or less than $\frac{1}{2}$. Students may need reminders to think about and use equivalent fractions to justify the sums of numbers that do not have a common denominator. Wherever possible, make connections to the work students did in the Visualize activity to support their thinking in this task.

Activity

Launch

Launch the lesson, if possible, by showing students some examples of Mondrian's paintings from the 1940s. You might ask them to turn and talk to a partner about what they notice about these paintings. Take some observations from students, who might notice the colors and shapes used. Then show students the example they worked with in the Visualize activity that is modeled on Mondrian's work, Patches. Tell them that this is not a real Mondrian painting. It is meant to look like his paintings, but it was not made by him, so today we're going to think of it as a fake.

Ask students to again turn and talk to a partner about what they notice the fake and the real paintings have in common and how they are different. Have students share ideas. They might notice the color palettes' being similar. Be sure they notice that Mondrian's real paintings often contain a lot of white space and that the fake we looked at does not. This makes it a bad fake. Someone who knows Piet Mondrian's work well would be able to detect that it is not real. Tell students that their job today is to make a good fake.

Explore

Students work in partners to create a convincing fake Mondrian painting. Students can decide to modify the fake painting provided or to start over and design from scratch. Mondrian's paintings are typically no more than $\frac{1}{2}$ color. The remainder is usually white and black. To make a good fake, students need to make a painting that uses blue, yellow, and red so that these colors are no more than $\frac{1}{2}$ of the painting. After students have created their fake, have them answer the following questions on their Analyzing Our Fake sheet:

- What fraction of the painting is each color?
- How do you know that the three colors together are less that $\frac{1}{2}$ of the painting? Prove your results both visually and with numbers.

After students have made one good fake and analyzed it, ask students to make a fake that is close but not accurate—where the colors are just a little more than $\frac{1}{2}$—and analyze it on a second sheet.

Discuss

Before the whole-class discussion, ask students to post their different paintings around the room, both the good fakes and any close fakes students may have created. Make sure that the good fakes and close fakes are mixed together. Have partnerships go around the room together, as in a gallery walk, and verify several paintings to see whether they meet our constraints. Is it a good fake? Ask, Can you spot the close fakes? Students need to be ready to prove their findings. You might want to provide sticky notes for students to post their evidence—and their determination, good fake or close fake—next to each painting.

Once students have had a chance to do some detective work, bring them together for a discussion of which paintings are good fakes and which fakes just don't work, and how they know. If there are any disagreements, make time to discuss evidence from both sides.

Then discuss how students went about making their paintings:

- What did you have to think about when you were making your fakes—either the good one or the close one?
- How did you use fractions to help you as you planned and created your paintings?

In all of these discussions, be sure to highlight ideas about fraction equivalence that help students add and subtract.

Look-Fors

- **Are students thinking in fractions, or in squares?** Students may use the unit of the square on the dot paper (see appendix) or original fake painting, find how many there are, and then simply think about how many squares to use or leave white. Although this strategy will work, it may then be difficult for students to complete their painting analysis in which they need to justify why the three color fractions sum to less than $\frac{1}{2}$. Challenge students to reframe their thinking about their painting in terms of fractions to help them justify what they have created—rather than starting over. Knowing how many squares there are is just a step away from thinking about what the unit fraction is, which will in turn help students name the fraction of any region.

- **How are students writing number sentences to represent and prove their work?** This is an important part of the learning in this lesson, in which students connect their visual work to more abstract fraction representations. Students may encounter difficulty in adding together their fractions if they are named with different denominators, such as $\frac{13}{100}$, $\frac{1}{10}$, and $\frac{1}{4}$. Remind students of the work they did in the Visualize activity by referring back to the charts they created in that lesson. You might ask students: How could equivalent fractions help you add? What equivalent fractions would be useful?

- **How are students justifying whether a fraction is more or less than $\frac{1}{2}$?** Many students struggle to estimate the approximate value of fractions using benchmarks, even those as well-known as $\frac{1}{2}$. If they see a fraction such as $\frac{47}{100}$, students many struggle to understand its relationship to $\frac{1}{2}$, and they may struggle even more if the denominator is odd, such as $\frac{12}{25}$. Ask students: What fraction would be color if it were exactly $\frac{1}{2}$? How can knowing that help you think about whether your fraction is more or less than $\frac{1}{2}$? Some students, particularly those working with an odd denominator, might benefit from drawing a picture that is the same size as the one they have created and marking out $\frac{1}{2}$ clearly so that they can see what it looks like and compare.

Reflect

If you were given two fractions to add, such as $\frac{3}{5}$ and $\frac{1}{6}$, what would you have to think about in order to find their sum?

 **Patches**

Inspired by *Composition II in Red, Blue, and Yellow,* by Piet Mondrian, 1921.

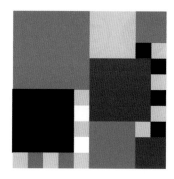

What fraction of the painting is each color?

How do you know that the three colors together are less than (or a little more than) $\frac{1}{2}$ of the painting? Prove your results both visually and with numbers.

Squares with a Difference

Snapshot

Students bring together their understanding of fraction equivalence and fraction addition and subtraction to investigate partitioning squares and comparing the regions inside.

Connection to CCSS
5.NF.1
5.NF.2

Agenda

Activity	Time	Description/Prompt	Materials
Launch	10 min	Introduce students to partitioning by asking them to examine a 2 × 2 square that has been divided into smaller regions. Use this square to describe the investigation today.	• 2 × 2 Square sheet, to display • Chart and markers
Explore	30+ min	Partners investigate how to partition squares of different sizes (2 × 2, 3 × 3, . . . 10 × 10) into rectangles and color them so that the difference between the blue and yellow regions is $\frac{1}{4}$. Students try to find as many solutions as possible and identify what size squares have solutions and which do not.	• Square Grids sheets, multiple copies per partnership • Square tiles in yellow, blue, and other colors • Colors • Grid paper (see appendix), as needed
Discuss	15+ min	Discuss students' findings, including their strategies, their solutions, and which size squares had no solutions. Look for patterns that can help students understand what works and why.	Chart and markers

(Continued)

Activity	Time	Description/Prompt	Materials
Explore	30+ min	Partners return to the investigation, now exploring creating a difference between the yellow and blue regions that is $\frac{1}{3}$. What size squares have solutions now? What size squares have no solutions and why? Students continue their investigation by looking at other unit fraction differences of their choosing.	• Square Grids sheets, multiple copies per partnership • Square tiles in yellow, blue, and other colors • Colors • Grid paper (see appendix), as needed
Discuss	20+ min	Create a class display of the different solutions for all square sizes and the fraction differences of $\frac{1}{3}$, $\frac{1}{4}$, and any others that students investigated. Use this display to discuss patterns and determine why some sizes work for a given fraction.	Class-created display of solutions

To the Teacher

In this investigation, students will be exploring partitioning squares into rectangular regions and coloring them so that there is a given difference between two regions, the blue and the yellow. We begin with a difference of $\frac{1}{4}$ and then proceed to investigate other unit fraction differences. Student look at squares of different sizes, beginning with a 2×2 square and continuing through a 10×10. This investigation involves lots of thinking about fraction equivalence and fraction difference, as well as factors and multiples. Launching this investigation with clarity is critical, as it involves thinking about fractions and area models differently than students are likely to have done in the past. Be sure that students see that they are looking to create a *difference* of $\frac{1}{4}$, which is to say that one region is $\frac{1}{4}$ greater (or less) than the other. Students won't be able to see $\frac{1}{4}$ on the grid in the way they may anticipate, because it is the difference between two regions, not the regions themselves. It may help students if you point to the example in the launch and ask, Where is the $\frac{1}{4}$ difference? Students will need to see it as the part of the blue region that is greater than the yellow. One additional parameter that needs to be clear is that students must partition the squares along the grid lines, which is to say that the regions must have whole-number side lengths. All square sizes work if students ignore the grid lines; by using the grid lines, we explore fraction equivalence and its utility in depth.

This investigation will take at least two days, and we encourage you not to rush. Students will work at different paces and will need time to collect enough evidence to begin to see patterns. Some students may have their own ideas for extending the investigation, such as exploring larger squares (say, 11×11 or 12×12). If students have gathered sufficient evidence to identify some patterns they want to explore, we encourage you to let them extend their investigation. The longer students investigate, and the larger their squares become, the more paper resources students will need.

Activity

Launch

Tell students that mathematicians have been studying how to partition areas and what patterns they can make in partitioned shapes for a long time. Partitioning is cutting a shape into smaller parts. Today we're going to investigate partitioning, too. We're going to look at how to partition squares so that there is a particular difference between two of the areas inside of it. Let's look at an example of a 2 × 2 square that has been partitioned into rectangles.

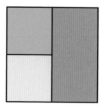

Ask students, What is the difference between the fraction of area that is blue and the fraction of area that is yellow? Give students a moment to turn and talk to a partner. Be sure students are thinking in fractions of the whole, rather than in squares (that is, $\frac{1}{2} - \frac{1}{4}$ instead of $2 - 1$).

Show students the empty square below it on the 2 × 2 Square sheet. Ask, Is there a different way we could partition this square so that the difference between the blue and yellow areas is still $\frac{1}{4}$? Tell students that this is a 2 × 2 square and that for today's work, we must partition along whole numbers of units. Give students a moment to turn and talk to a partner, then ask for ideas. Chart any contributions students may have. It is important to use this example as a place for students to brainstorm and see other possibilities before they go off to work on the investigation. Students might see that they can split up the blue portion into two smaller squares and the difference between the yellow and blue would remain the same, or that they can swap which color is the larger region (that is, yellow could take up $\frac{1}{2}$ of the square and blue could be $\frac{1}{4}$).

Tell students that in today's investigation, they will be partitioning squares of lots of different sizes into rectangular areas and deciding how to color them in so that the difference between the fraction that is blue and the fraction that is yellow is still $\frac{1}{4}$. Ask, What different ways can we do this? How many solutions can we find? Can we find solutions for any size square?

Explore

Provide students with square tiles (blue and yellow and at least one other color), Square Grids sheets, grid paper (see appendix), and colors. Students work with a partner to investigate the question, How can you partition squares of different sizes into rectangles and color them so that the difference between the yellow and blue areas is $\frac{1}{4}$?

- What are the different ways you can find to solve this problem?
- What size squares work?
- What size squares do not work? Why?

Encourage students to label their different solutions with number sentences to help them remember what they were thinking. They will work with many squares, and labels will support students in organizing, remembering, and reporting their work.

Discuss

Gather students together to discuss the different solutions they found for a difference of $\frac{1}{4}$. Chart solutions, observations, patterns, and questions that students generated during this first part of the investigation.

- How did you have to think about the fractions to find a difference of $\frac{1}{4}$?
- What different ways did you find to partition squares?
- What patterns were you using to help you? What patterns did you notice?
- What size squares did we find solutions for? Which sizes did we not find solutions for? Why do you think that is?

Then ask students: What do you think will happen if, instead, you were trying to make a difference of $\frac{1}{3}$, or some other unit fraction? Do you think the same size squares would have solutions? Give students a moment to turn and talk to make a prediction, then introduce the next part of the investigation.

Explore

Ask student partnerships to investigate what solutions they can find for partitioning squares of different sizes into rectangles and coloring them so that the difference between the blue and yellow regions is $\frac{1}{3}$.

- What are the different ways you can find to solve this problem?
- What size squares work?
- What size squares do not work? Why?
- How are your solutions similar to those you found for $\frac{1}{4}$? How are they different? Why?

Students can investigate other unit fractions, such as $\frac{1}{5}$ or $\frac{1}{6}$, to look for patterns in their solutions. Ask, Can you predict what size squares will work for a fraction before you begin? For each unit fraction students investigate, ask them to record their findings on a separate Square Grids sheet or piece of grid paper (see appendix) to help them organize their solutions for sharing. See Figures 3.1 and 3.2 for examples of student work. Our Square Grids sheet ends with 10 × 10 squares, but students might also want to extend their investigation beyond this size, which they can do by making their own squares on grid paper (see appendix).

Discuss

Gather students together with their solutions. Because students will have investigated different fraction differences, you'll need a way to pool all the solutions students

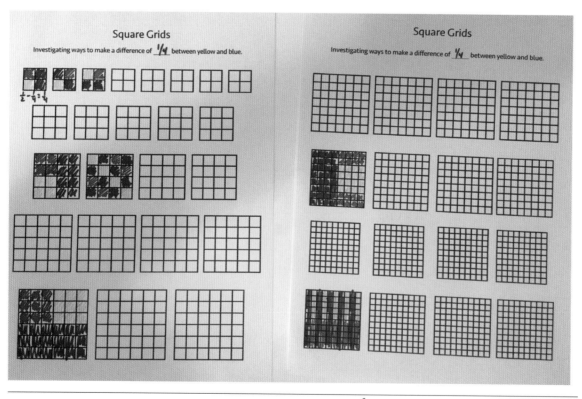

Figure 3.1   Student Work in Progress Finding a Difference of $\frac{1}{4}$

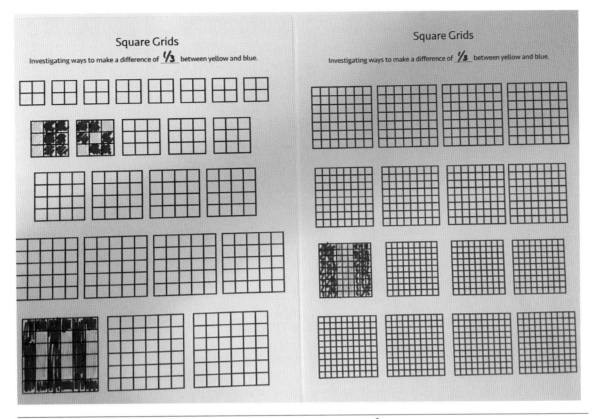

Figure 3.2   Student Work in Progress Finding a Difference of $\frac{1}{3}$

found so that the class can look for patterns across them. We suggest that you ask students how the class could organize their findings to see patterns about what size squares work and what size squares don't work for the fraction differences they investigated. Support students in developing a class organizational system. You might find that a table on a bulletin board or wall is useful, similar to the one in Figure 3.3.

Once you have your organizing system in place, use it to collect students' solutions and figure out why some square sizes work for some differences and others don't. You may want students to reproduce their solutions on cut-out pieces of grid paper (see appendix) so that they can be posted for all to see, which you can also use to honor the many different solutions students may have come up with for a given fraction and square size. This can also serve as a source for additional inquiry: Why do some of the square sizes with solutions have many solutions while others have few? If students are not yet confident or need more data, send them back to gather more information through additional investigation.

	2x2	3x3	4x4	5x5	6x6	7x7	8x8	9x9	10x10
1/3		✓			✓			✓	
1/4	✓		✓		✓		✓		✓
1/5									
1/6									

Figure 3.3   Sample Table for Recording Student Data

Look-Fors

- **Are students clear about what the fraction in this problem represents?**
  Critical to this investigation is the idea of a fraction *difference*. Some students
  may struggle with this idea because when they look at an area model, they
  may expect to be able to see $\frac{1}{4}$ shaded in somewhere; this is how we typically
  use area models when teaching fractions. But in this investigation, we suggest that $\frac{1}{4}$ is the difference between two areas, not a region that students can
  touch. It may support some students to think about this as one region being
  $\frac{1}{4}$ more than another, or that if they subtracted the smaller region from the
  larger one, then they would see $\frac{1}{4}$ remaining. Start these conversations simply
  by asking, What does it mean that there is a *difference* of $\frac{1}{4}$ between the blue
  and the yellow? This question will help you uncover the confusion, if it exists,
  and then you can clarify the parameters of the task.

- **How are students getting started?** Some students may design a partitioned square and then struggle to determine how to get started coloring

and adjusting the regions so that the difference between the blue and yellow regions is $\frac{1}{4}$ (or whatever fraction was their goal). Encourage students to partition their square in some way, start testing ideas, and recording the results using number sentences. This record will support students in beginning to see patterns that enable them to think ahead about the fractions that might make sense. Once students start seeing patterns, they will likely start in different places when thinking about solving these puzzles. For instance, some students will start by thinking about the larger region first and then thinking about taking away $\frac{1}{4}$ to see what is left. Other students will think about $\frac{1}{4}$, find an equivalent fraction for the square size (say, $\frac{1}{4} = \frac{4}{16}$ for a 4×4 square), and then use that to generate fraction pairs that are $\frac{1}{4}$ apart. These strategies only emerge through students' trying lots of squares first and using the recorded number sentences and diagrams to look for patterns in what works, what gets close, and what doesn't work.

- **How are students using their trials to get closer?** Some students may try partitioning and coloring on a grid, find that their trial doesn't work, and get frustrated having to start over each time. Especially at the beginning of this investigation, when students will be making lots of mistakes and may still be trying to figure out what this investigation requires, students may benefit from using square tiles instead of the grids. The square tiles enable students to swap one square out for a different color easily so that adjustments feel fluid. Ask students to record the solutions they find and any trials that don't work that they think might be useful evidence for a square being impossible. As students gain confidence, they may move to using the grids on their own.

- **Are students getting stuck on a single square (perhaps without a solution)? Are students dismissing squares as impossible too quickly?** Some students may get stuck searching and searching for a solution to a square that doesn't have one; others may make one effort on a square that does not work and then dismiss that square as impossible. The key questions here are: How do you know when a square will never work? Why is it that some sizes do not work for some fraction differences? For some students, thinking about these questions will help them see that there is a real mathematical barrier to finding a solution and enable them to move on. For other students, you might want to push them to stick with the square until they gather enough evidence to be certain.

- **How are students keeping track of their work?** Students will be working across many different square sizes and looking for differences of $\frac{1}{4}$ and $\frac{1}{3}$ and perhaps others. This investigation will generate a lot of squares to keep track of, and some students may begin to get confused about what they have tried, what worked and didn't, how they know, and what squares were meant to explore the different fractions. Labels are hugely helpful in organizing the work and, ultimately, seeing patterns. Encourage students to label their work with the fraction difference they are investigating and to label each square with a number sentence. Students need to develop some way of indicating trials that don't work and those that are successful solutions. Students should keep records even of the trials that do not work, because these can be evidence for squares that are impossible, and they can be useful when comparing their own thinking to that of others.

Reflect

Where can you see equivalent fractions in this investigation? How might they help you think about the squares that do and do not work for a particular fraction difference?

 **2 × 2 Square**

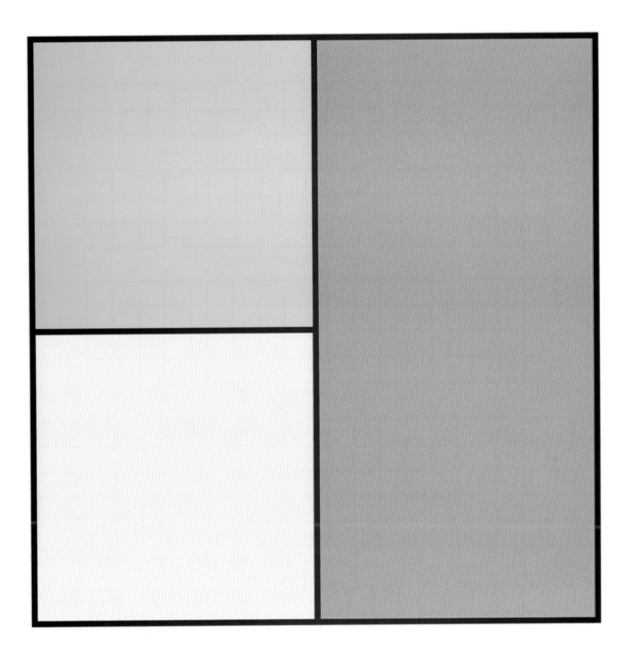

Square Grids

Investigating ways to make a difference of _____ between yellow and blue.

 **Square Grids**

Investigating ways to make a difference of _____ between yellow and blue.

Exploring the Coordinate Plane

Coordinate planes enable us to do something that is really mathematically interesting and cool: record, with one small point, two different dimensions of an object. But, as with all mathematical ideas, when the concept is taught as a set of rules about ways to record accurately, the coolness can disappear for students. A really nice way to introduce coordinate graphs to students is to have them use the main idea without recording numbers. The activity that we share in our Visualize activity is one that we introduced to students in our Youcubed summer camp. Part of the three-minute film that demonstrates the impact of the camp shows the students working on this activity on whiteboards: www.youcubed.org/resources/solving-math-problem/

We asked students to look at a graph and then to make one of their own. We asked them to choose the topic of their graph and what they would measure on their axes. This was a really interesting and engaging activity for students and one that focused them on the meaning of coordinate graphs, not the technical details that would come later.

Many mathematical ideas can be shared on a coordinate plane. Our Youcubed video of mathematical connections www.youcubed.org/resources/tour-mathematical-connections/ shows the ways fractions can be illustrated on a coordinate plane to reveal their relationships. In our investigation, we invited students to plot the patterns they saw in the multiplication table on a coordinate plane. When we were investigating the multiplication table ourselves and we saw the arcs that are revealed when we color in the same number that appears in different places (Figure 4.1), we were enthralled, and we thought students would be too.

Multiplication Table

X	1	2	3	4	5	6	7	8	9	10	11	12	13	14	15	16
1	1	2	3	4	5	6	7	8	9	10	11	12	13	14	15	16
2	2	4	6	8	10	12	14	16	18	20	22	24	26	28	30	32
3	3	6	9	12	15	18	21	24	27	30	33	36	39	42	45	48
4	4	8	12	16	20	24	28	32	36	40	44	48	52	56	60	64
5	5	10	15	20	25	30	35	40	45	50	55	60	65	70	75	80
6	6	12	18	24	30	36	42	48	54	60	66	72	78	84	90	96
7	7	14	21	28	35	42	49	56	63	70	77	84	91	98	105	112
8	8	16	24	32	40	48	56	64	72	80	88	96	104	112	120	128
9	9	18	27	36	45	54	63	72	81	90	99	108	117	126	135	144
10	10	20	30	40	50	60	70	80	90	100	110	120	130	140	150	160
11	11	22	33	44	55	66	77	88	99	110	121	132	143	154	165	176
12	12	24	36	48	60	72	84	96	108	120	132	144	156	168	180	192
13	13	26	39	52	65	78	91	104	117	130	143	156	169	182	195	208
14	14	28	42	56	70	84	98	112	126	140	154	168	182	196	210	224
15	15	30	45	60	75	90	105	120	135	150	165	180	195	210	225	240
16	16	32	48	64	80	96	112	128	144	160	176	192	208	224	240	256

For the lesson in this book, we have combined the activity of looking for patterns in the table with the task of plotting them on a coordinate graph. The activities that make up this big idea all invite students to think about what is being represented by the coordinate plane, not just plot points with no meaning, and to engage with coordinate planes through interesting activities that they will need to think about deeply.

In our Visualize activity, we share a graph with points plotted without numbers so that the students can think about what they mean. We first got this idea from a graph of fruit that Randall Munroe developed and Dan Meyer shared and then put onto Desmos. It is a really nice way to introduce students to coordinate planes. After sharing an example with students, we ask them to come up with their own ideas and to make their own four-quadrant graph.

In our Play activity, students are invited to play a game similar to Battleship, in which they need to think about particular points on the graph. This fun and engaging activity is a nice way to introduce students to the precise location of points on a graph. The game also offers students a chance to be strategic in their game play and for you to highlight the value of strategic choices that are based on feedback.

In our Investigate activity, we invite students to do something that is always mathematically worthwhile: explore patterns in the multiplication table. The arcs shown in the earlier graphic are just one type of interesting pattern that students may discover and explore. We also give them the opportunity to consider the ways that the multiplication table is similar to or different from the coordinate plane. This will give them a chance to see that the coordinate plane communicates information through points that are located at the intersection of the different grid lines. As with all of our Investigate activities, we hope that students will feel free to explore, pursuing mathematical patterns and ideas that are interesting to them.

Jo Boaler

Getting around the Plane

Snapshot

Students explore the meaning of the coordinate plane by interpreting and creating four-quadrant graphs, using qualitative comparisons instead of values on the axes.

Connection to CCSS
5.G.1
5.G.2

Agenda

Activity	Time	Description/Prompt	Materials
Launch	15 min	The class examines a four-quadrant graph showing modes of transportation, where one axis represents speed (fast vs. slow) and the other represents enjoyment (fun vs. not fun). Students discuss their interpretations of the graph.	• Four-Quadrant Transportation Graph to show students • Optional: copies of the Four-Quadrant Transportation Graph for partners, chart, and markers
Explore	30 min	Groups create their own four-quadrant graph on a poster, comparing two dimensions of a topic they choose. Groups must agree on where to place the data points on their graph.	Chart and markers for each group
Discuss	15–20 min	Groups swap graphs and discuss interpretations of another group's graph. Students mark with sticky notes any points that raise questions or spark disagreement. Groups then present the graph they explored and any questions it raised. Discuss what the graphs enable students to communicate and see.	• Posters from each group • Sticky notes

To the Teacher

This activity engages students in thinking about the relationships the coordinate plane can communicate. Whereas fifth graders are typically asked only to work with the first quadrant, and later zoom out to think about all four quadrants, we think it makes more sense to first give students an experience with the whole coordinate plane. To ensure that students focus on relationships—not integers—this lesson centers on dimensions without measures. In the example graph used in the launch, one dimension, speed, could be quantified, but we choose simply to express it qualitatively as fast or slow. The other dimension, enjoyment, cannot be measured and is subjective. The qualitative and subjective nature of these measurements can generate productive disagreement and debate about the placement of individual data points. Students may well dispute where on the plane we have placed, for instance, the subway, depending on how rare or typical, exciting or ordinary riding the subway is for them. We think this is a great opportunity for students to engage with the meanings in a coordinate plane, rather than simply plotting points.

Activity

Launch

Launch this activity by showing students the Four-Quadrant Transportation Graph on a projector. You may want to hand out copies for students to examine with a partner. Without explaining what the graph shows, ask students to make some observations, generate interpretations, and ask questions. Ask: What do you notice? What does the graph show? What do the individual points mean? What does the graph make you wonder? Give students some time to turn and talk to a partner, as needed, to think aloud about what the graph shows. As you discuss the meanings in the graph, record students' thinking on a chart or by annotating the graph itself. Be sure to engage students in thinking about the relationships the graph communicates, that each point shows both how fast and how fun the mode of transportation is to the person who created the graph.

After students have begun to form interpretations of the graph, ask whether there are any points on the graph that students disagree with. Invite discussion and debate. You may want to revise the graph to reflect where your class thinks the points should be placed. If there is a form of transportation used by students (or one they can imagine) that is not shown, you might ask them to discuss where it should be placed and then add that data point to the graph.

Ask students to notice how the graph is set up. Take some observations. Students should notice that the two axes each have opposites indicated at the far ends. Introduce today's task to the class. Be sure to talk with students about the need for a topic and two dimensions, one for each axis, where two different qualities exist (such as fun vs. not fun, fast vs. slow). Before sending them to their groups to begin work, you may want to offer students an opportunity to turn and talk with a partner to brainstorm the kinds of topics that could be graphed.

Explore

Students work in small groups to create their own four-quadrant graph using different axis labels and a different topic from the one used in the launch. Students should brainstorm several ideas before settling on a topic, and they should consider what the dimensions being compared on the graph could be. The group must agree on both the topic and the dimensions of comparison before constructing their graph.

Each group will construct a graph on chart paper, clearly labeling the topic and axes. Ask students to come up with several points to place on the graph (for example, subway, car, bike). Students must agree on the placement of each point. Students can use symbols, as in the transportation graph, or labeled points for their data.

Discuss

Each group swaps graphs with another group. As they swap, ask groups not to share any details except what is on the graph. Ask students to look at the graph they receive and discuss within their group how they interpret the graph. Provide students with sticky notes for recording their interpretations of the graph, questions they have, and any points they disagree with and why.

Have each group present the poster they just explored (rather than the one they made). The presenting group would also share its questions about the graph. Let the group who made the graph offer any clarification at the end.

As a class, discuss the following questions:

- What does a four-quadrant graph enable you to communicate? What can you learn from this kind of graph?
- What made placing your data points challenging for your group? What disagreements came up?

Look-Fors

- **Are students choosing dimensions with two clear distinctions to give their axes meaning?** Because the graphs students are creating in this activity do not have numerical values for the axes, the dimensions they choose to compare must have two distinct qualities. We have shown fast vs. slow and fun vs. not fun, but many other possibilities exist. Students might use dimensions such as delicious vs. not delicious, easy vs. hard, common vs. rare, or awesome vs. not awesome.

- **Are students considering both the relationship between the axes and the relationship between the points when placing their data?** Placing a data point on the graph is first a matter of considering each dimension: left or right, up or down, extreme or close to the center. But as students accumulate points on the graph, they must also consider how each new point fits compared to the other points already on the graph. For instance, if students were placing roller skating on the transportation graph, they would need to consider not just whether it is fast, but also how much faster or slower it is than biking. Looking at the graphs students construct, ask probing questions about the placement and inquire about the relationship between the points to encourage students to think about those relationships and to revise as needed.

- **Are students noticing relationships when interpreting graphs?** These four-quadrant graphs communicate a web of relationships, between the two axes and between the various points on the graph. When students are looking at graphs made by others, encourage them to think about the points individually and in relationship to one another. These relationships may well spark questions and disagreement, which are both useful ways to engage with the ideas in the graph.

Reflect

What other topics would you like to see graphed on a four-quadrant graph? What would the axes be? What would you be interested to learn from this graph?

Four-Quadrant Transportation Graph

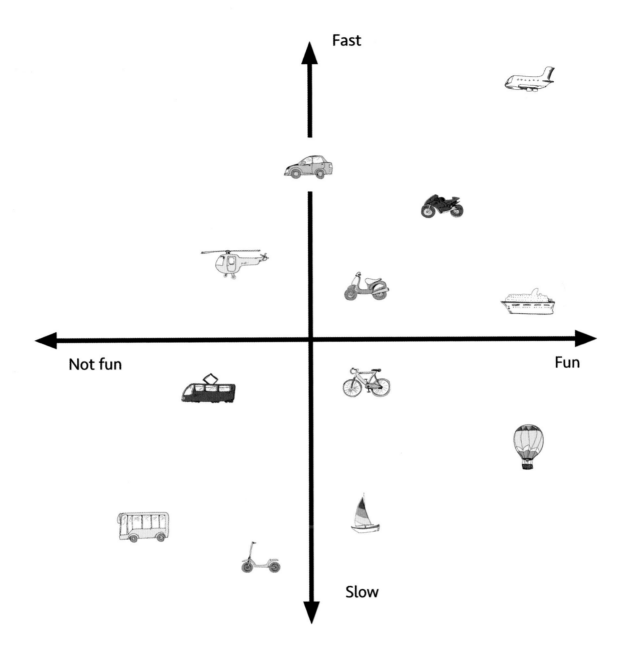

Ship Shape

Snapshot

Students play with describing and locating points—and the shapes they make—in the first quadrant of the coordinate plane in a game called Ship Shape.

Connection to CCSS
5.G.1
5.G.2

Agenda

Activity	Time	Description/Prompt	Materials
Launch	15 min	Students look at a rectangle on a coordinate plane and develop ways to describe its location. The class agrees on clear and precise descriptions. Name the convention of describing points at (x, y). Describe the directions for playing Ship Shape.	Where Is the Rectangle? graph, to display
Play	30 min	Partners play Ship Shape, in which they each hide a group of shapes on their own coordinate plane and then take turns trying to guess where those same shapes are hidden on their partner's plane.	• Ship Shape Game Sheets, two per player for each round • File folders, one per player
Discuss	10–15 min	Discuss strategies students developed for locating shapes and recording the results of the guesses on their coordinate planes.	
Extend	30+ min	Partners design and test their own Ship Shape Game Sheets, with the goal of creating a set of shapes that is more interesting or challenging to play with.	• Make Your Own Ship Shape Game Sheets, multiple copies per player • File folders, one per player

To the Teacher

In today's game, we move from developing a holistic sense of the relationships represented in all four quadrants of the coordinate plane in the Visualize lesson to taking a close and precise look at the first quadrant. In this lesson, we use locating shapes on the coordinate plane as a way of introducing and practicing with the conventions we have for describing the location of points on the coordinate plane. Students also get some experience with attending to the sides and angles of a group of polygons and trying some transformational geometry as they plot, slide, and rotate the shapes.

We have provided two different game sheets for this game, one with four shapes and one with six. We recommend starting with the board with four shapes, and students can move to the board with six for later rounds. We have also provided a blank game sheet for the extension, in which partners create and test their own game boards. If students develop a set of shapes that they think works well as an interesting game sheet, you might photocopy their boards to make it easier for others to try them out or play repeatedly.

Activity

Launch

Launch this activity by showing students the Where Is the Rectangle? graph on a projector. Ask students, How could we describe where this rectangle is to someone who couldn't see the graph? Ask students to turn and talk to a partner about this question. Then take student descriptions and scribe them on a chart or board. Pay attention to when students use the numbers on the axes to locate or when they attend to the vertices. When students use the axis labels, ask why they chose this as a clear way of describing the location of the rectangle or its vertices. You may also want to ask why the vertices are features of the rectangle that help locate it on the graph. These two ideas, that the vertices describe the shape and that the axis labels can locate points, are critical to this lesson and using the coordinate plane.

You might ask the class to look at all the contributions for how to describe the rectangle's location and ask, Which of these descriptions do we think is the clearest? The most efficient? Name for students the convention for locating points on the coordinate plane: (x, y). Try using this language together by giving students three points: $(2, 3)$, $(6, 3)$, and $(6, 5)$. Ask students to discuss with a partner what kind of triangle is made by these points and where it would be on the graph. You may want to invite students to come up and place these points on the graph and see the right triangle created.

Tell students that today they will be playing a game with a partner using this way of locating points and shapes on the coordinate plane. Introduce the game Ship Shape by showing students the materials and describing the directions.

Play

Ship Shape is played in pairs. Each student will need two copies of Ship Shape Game Sheet 1 and a file folder. Partners will need to position themselves across from one another with file folders standing up to keep their game sheets private.

Game Directions

- Each partner gets two sheets, one to record their hunt for their partner's shapes and the other to hide their own shapes. Partners each use a file folder to separate their planes from each other.

- Before play begins, each partner must hide all of the shapes shown on the right side of the game sheet on their own coordinate plane by drawing. Players may rotate the shapes when they place them, but not change their size or shape. Players mark the shapes clearly on the plane.
- Partners then begin play by taking turns guessing points on the coordinate plane, with the goal of finding a vertex of one of the shapes. Players should use the (x, y) convention in naming points.
  - If a vertex is found, the partner says, "Nailed it!"
  - If a point on a side or inside the shape is found, the partner says, "Ping!"
  - If the point is outside of any shapes, the partner says, "Missed!"
  - When all the vertices of a shape have been found, the partner says, "You found my triangle [square, trapezoid, and so on]."
- Players should develop ways to record the results of their guesses on their sheets.
- The first person to find all their partner's shapes wins.

Students may play multiple rounds, and will need new game sheets for each round. After students have played with the game board with four shapes, they may want to try the board with six shapes.

Discuss

After students have had a chance to play at least one full round, gather them together to discuss the following questions:

- What strategies did you come up with to help you find shapes?
- What was challenging about finding the shapes on the coordinate plane?
- How did you record the results of your guesses to keep track of where shapes might or might not be?

Extend

Partners can make their own shape set using the blank Make Your Own Ship Shape Game Sheet. Ask students, What kinds of shapes can you make that will make it more challenging or interesting to play? Students may want to create and test a variety of game sheets to develop an interesting or challenging game that others could play. You may want to photocopy students' final designs so that they can swap with other groups and play.

Look-Fors

- **Are students using the (x, y) convention to name points on the coordinate plane?** Listen in as students name points, and watch them mark the feedback on their boards. The use of (x, y) in that order is simply a mathematical convention, and students are not expected to be fluent with this convention immediately. They may well flip the order, which you will be able to see if they call a value (x, y) and then mark it on their plane as (y, x). This is an instance where it makes sense simply to remind students of the convention by referring to the charts you created during the launch.

- **Are students changing the shapes when they place them on the coordinate plane?** The game is far more interesting if students rotate or flip the shapes when placing them on the coordinate plane before the game begins. This can be challenging work, as it requires attending to the relationships between the vertices and transforming them as they transform the shape. Students may make mistakes that change the angles or side lengths as they try to plot the shapes. Encourage students to compare their placed shape to the original and ask how they know the two are congruent.

- **Are students thinking strategically about the feedback they get from their guesses?** Encourage students to move from random guesses—which they must use in the beginning of each game—to thinking strategically about their next guess. Each guess should give the student some feedback, and any guess that gets a "Ping!" for being on a side or inside the shape should lead to nearby guesses next. As students locate vertices, they should be able to hypothesize about which shape they may have found and where the other vertices may be. You may want to slow students' game down and ask them to think aloud about what they know and what the best guesses will be. This is a game in which revealing your strategy or pondering it aloud does not compromise your chance of winning, because the shapes are already placed and cannot be moved.

Reflect

How can you imagine people using or seeing a coordinate plane in real life?

Where Is the Rectangle?

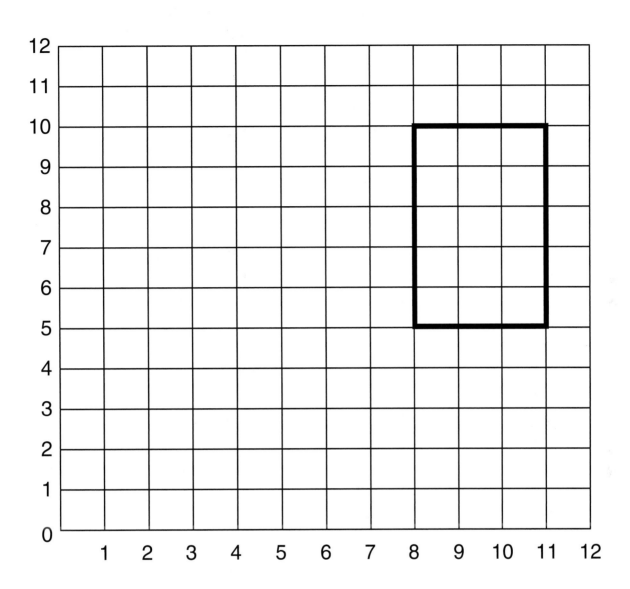

Ship Shape Game Sheet 1

Found a vertex? Say, "Nailed it!"

Landed on the perimeter or inside? Say, "Ping!"

Landed on the empty plane? Say, "Missed!"

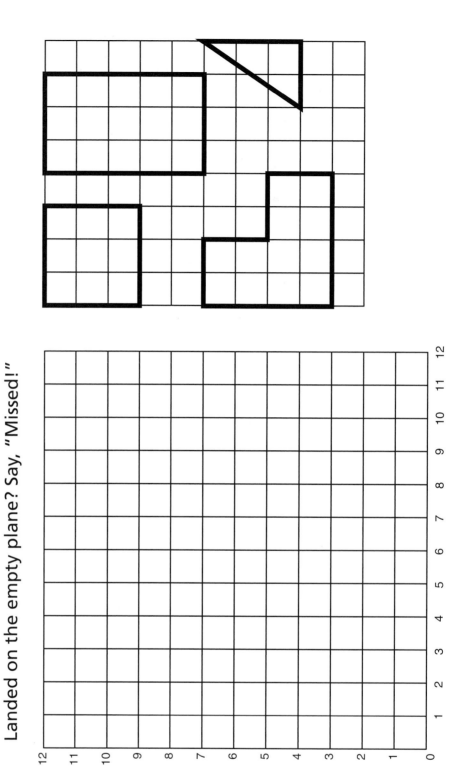

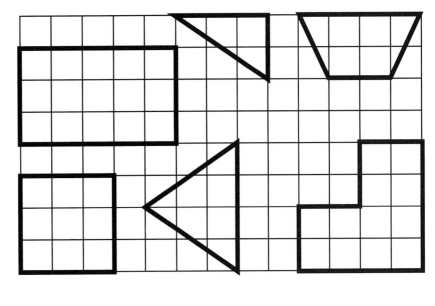

Ship Shape Game Sheet 2

Found a vertex? Say, "Nailed it!"

Landed on the perimeter or inside? Say, "Ping!"

Landed on the empty plane? Say, "Missed!"

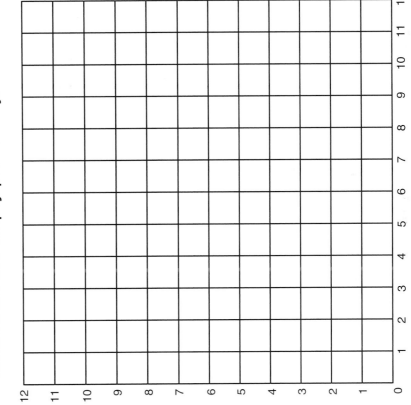

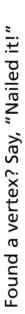

Make Your Own Ship Shape Game Sheet

Found a vertex? Say, "Nailed it!"

Landed on the perimeter or inside? Say, "Ping!"

Landed on the empty plane? Say, "Missed!"

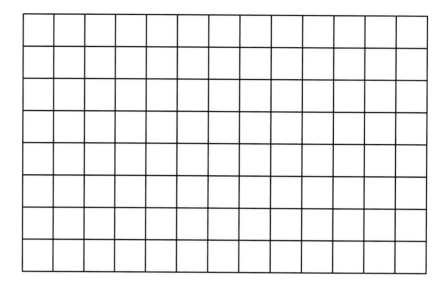

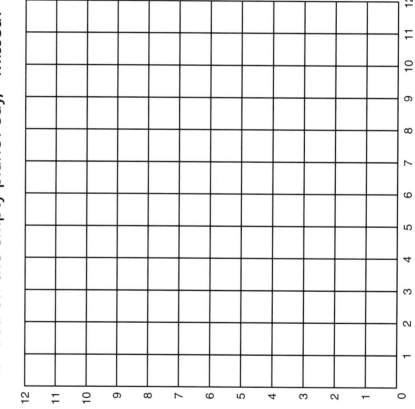

Table Patterns

Snapshot

Students explore patterns in the multiplication table and then investigate what happens when they graph those patterns on the coordinate plane.

Connection to CCSS
5.G.1
5.G.2

Agenda

Activity	Time	Description/Prompt	Materials
Launch	5–10 min	Show students a partially complete multiplication table and ask them what patterns they notice. Collect student observations and point out that several values appear repeatedly, whereas others appear only once or twice. Tell students they will investigate the repeating values.	Multiplication Table sheet, to display
Explore	20 min	Partners color-code repeating values in the multiplication table, extending the table to explore the patterns they create on the table.	• Multiplication Table sheet, one per student • Colors
Discuss	15+ min	Discuss the patterns students found in the repeating values on the multiplication table and their conjectures about these patterns. Compare the multiplication table to the coordinate plane.	• Students' color-coded Multiplication Table sheets • Multiplication Table sheet, to display • Coordinate Plane sheet, to display
Explore	20–30 min	Partners investigate how to show on the coordinate plane the patterns they found on the multiplication table. Partners test the class's conjectures by looking beyond what they found in the multiplication table.	• Students' work on the Multiplication Table sheets • Coordinate Plane sheet, one per student • Colors

(Continued)

Activity	Time	Description/Prompt	Materials
Discuss	15 min	Discuss how students represented the multiplication table patterns on the coordinate plane and what this representation enables them to see. Discuss the conjectures tested and how points, products, and area are related.	

To the Teacher

In this investigation, we draw connections between the multiplication table students have seen for years and the coordinate plane. Numbers we consider to be flexible appear often on the multiplication table: 12, 24, 36, and so on. Other numbers appear only once (such as 25) or twice (such as 7). In this investigation, we ask students to explore the repeating values and how they are arranged physically on the multiplication table, and later on the coordinate plane. The arcs these repeating values make, like the ones shown in Figure 4.1, are related to the factor pairs and will always end near both axes where we would find 1 times the number itself.

Students may not see these arcs at first, and they are probably not accustomed to drawing lines across the multiplication table. Encourage them to think about the shape they make, once they have color-coded repeating values. Students may be more apt to think about shape when they move to the coordinate plane, which is one advantage of the plane and something you can discuss as a class.

Activity

Launch

Launch the lesson by showing students the partially completed Multiplication Table sheet. Ask students, What patterns do you notice in the table? Give them a moment to turn and talk to a partner, then take some student observations of patterns. They may notice the counting sequence in the first column and row, or the symmetry of the table. They may notice the square numbers along the central diagonal. Take all observations and give students the opportunity to come up and point to where the patterns they see are found in the table so that others can see them, too. You may want to mark or color-code the table to show the patterns students point out.

Tell students that one of the patterns in the table is that some numbers show up several times, whereas others appear in the table only once or twice. Tell students

Multiplication Table

X	1	2	3	4	5	6	7	8	9	10	11	12	13	14	15	16
1	1	2	3	4	5	6	7	8	9	10	11	12	13	14	15	16
2	2	4	6	8	10	12	14	16	18	20	22	24	26	28	30	32
3	3	6	9	12	15	18	21	24	27	30	33	36	39	42	45	48
4	4	8	12	16	20	24	28	32	36	40	44	48	52	56	60	64
5	5	10	15	20	25	30	35	40	45	50	55	60	65	70	75	80
6	6	12	18	24	30	36	42	48	54	60	66	72	78	84	90	96
7	7	14	21	28	35	42	49	56	63	70	77	84	91	98	105	112
8	8	16	24	32	40	48	56	64	72	80	88	96	104	112	120	128
9	9	18	27	36	45	54	63	72	81	90	99	108	117	126	135	144
10	10	20	30	40	50	60	70	80	90	100	110	120	130	140	150	160
11	11	22	33	44	55	66	77	88	99	110	121	132	143	154	165	176
12	12	24	36	48	60	72	84	96	108	120	132	144	156	168	180	192
13	13	26	39	52	65	78	91	104	117	130	143	156	169	182	195	208
14	14	28	42	56	70	84	98	112	126	140	154	168	182	196	210	224
15	15	30	45	60	75	90	105	120	135	150	165	180	195	210	225	240
16	16	32	48	64	80	96	112	128	144	160	176	192	208	224	240	256

Figure 4.1   Arcs in the Multiplication Table

that today we are going to explore the numbers that seem to repeat and investigate the patterns they make in the table.

Explore

Students work in partners to color-code numbers that appear frequently in the multiplication table. Each student will need their own Multiplication Table sheet and colors. Students investigate the following questions:

- What values appear frequently in the table? Color-code the repeating values.
- Will these numbers continue to repeat? Extend the table as far as you'd like to investigate what happens beyond 8×8.
- How are repeating numbers arranged on the table?

- What conjectures can you make about what this pattern is showing and how you think the pattern might continue?

Discuss

Gather students together with their color-coded tables. Discuss the following questions:

- What values did you find repeated frequently in the table as you extended it?
- What did you notice about the patterns these values make on the table?
- What conjectures did you make about what the pattern is showing or how the pattern might continue?

After students have had the opportunity to share and perhaps notice the arcs made by repeating values in the multiplication table, display a fresh copy of the Multiplication Table sheet and a copy of the Coordinate Plane sheet. Ask students: How is the multiplication table like a coordinate plane? How are they different? Give students a few moments to turn and talk to a partner about the similarities and differences. Invite students to share their observations. You may want to mark what they notice on the two sheets, making connections between what is shared and highlighting differences.

One key difference we want students to see is that the numbers on the multiplication table align with the spaces—the blanks where we record the products—but in the coordinate plane, the values align with the grid lines. This means that on a coordinate plane, the numbers 3 and 6, for example, come together not inside a box but at the intersection of the two grid lines. If students do not point this out, you may want to ask them how the axis labels on the table and the plane are similar or different from each other to encourage them to attend to these features.

Ask students how they could show the patterns of repeating numbers they found in the multiplication table on the coordinate plane. You may want to give students a moment to turn and talk to their partner before giving them directions and sending them off to work.

Explore

Students work with their partner to investigate how to represent the patterns of repeating values in the multiplication table on the coordinate plane. Students will need their work from the first exploration, copies of the Coordinate Plane sheet, and colors. As students figure out how to place repeating values, such as 24, on the plane, ask students to think about how the coordinate plane shows 24. Ask, When you put this point on the graph, where is the 24?

Students may want to extend their graphs to include values and patterns they did not explore on the multiplication table, or to test the conjectures offered in the previous discussion. Encourage students to investigate, ask their own questions, and test ideas.

Discuss

Gather students with their graphs to discuss the following questions:

- What ways did you come up with for showing the multiplication patterns on the coordinate plane?
- What does the coordinate plane enable us to see? What do you notice that you hadn't before?
- What other repeating values did you locate? How were their patterns similar to or different from the ones we had already seen?
- Look at one set of similar values, say 24. How and where does the graph show the 24? How are the points (x, y) connected to the product? (You may want to highlight the observations students make, as in Figure 4.2.)
- Did anyone test one of the class conjectures? What did you find? Did the pattern continue as we expected? If not, what changed? Why?

Look-Fors

- **How are students completing the multiplication table?** Some students may just decide to fill in all the values at the beginning so that they can look across the whole table for repeating values. Other students may fill in the table in patches, with the idea that there may be a repeating value in a particular area. Ask questions about how these students are predicting where repeating values may appear. These hunches are the beginnings of conjectures.
- **Are students seeing the physical arrangement of repeating values on the multiplication table?** Students may be accustomed to seeing the multiplication table as rows and columns of skip counting, and are less experienced looking across the table. Students are often familiar with looking across the hundreds chart, where moving left and right, up and down, has concrete, countable meaning. Encourage students to approach looking at the multiplication table in a similar way. How do you move on the table from one 24 to another? Is it always the same? Why or why not? Is the pattern of 24s across

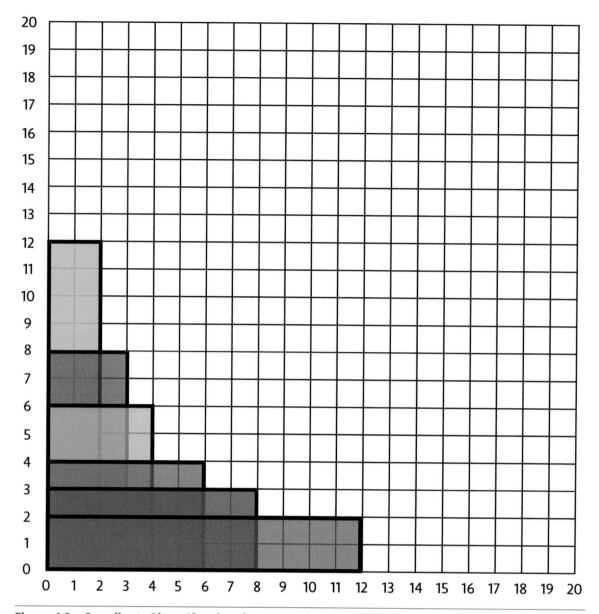

Figure 4.2   Coordinate Plane Showing the Rectangles of 24

the table the same as the pattern of 36s? Why or why not? Support students in getting curious about the arrangement of these values and what meaning underpins the pattern.

- **Are students locating points on the graph at the intersections of the lines?** The location of products is different on the multiplication table and the coordinate plane, moving from the box to the intersection of lines. Support students in noticing how the axes are labeled differently and what that means for locating points on the graph. You may want to remind students of work they did in the Play activity with naming the location of points, and ask students how they can use those ideas to map out repeating values on the plane.

- **Do students see a connection between the point, its product, and the area of the rectangle formed?** Each point on the coordinate plane is labeled with (x, y), and in the multiplication table we simply label the intersection with the product of $x \times y$. That product is the number of squares in the rectangle made by the origin and the point (x, y). For instance, the point $(9, 4)$ makes a rectangle 9×4 that starts in the origin and has an area of 36 squares. Encourage students to make connections between these different forms when they move to the coordinate plane. Asking students to label their points may support students in noticing connections.

Reflect

What other patterns in the multiplication table would you be interested to explore on the coordinate plane? What do you think they might look like?

Multiplication Table

×	1	2	3	4	5	6	7	8	9	10	11	12	13	14	15	16
1	1	2	3	4	5	6	7	8								
2	2	4	6	8	10	12	14	16								
3	3	6	9	12	15	18	21	24								
4	4	8	12	16	20	24	28	32								
5	5	10	15	20	25	30	35	40								
6	6	12	18	24	30	36	42	48								
7	7	14	21	28	35	42	49	56								
8	8	16	24	32	40	48	56	64								
9																
10																
11																
12																
13																
14																
15																
16																

Coordinate Plane

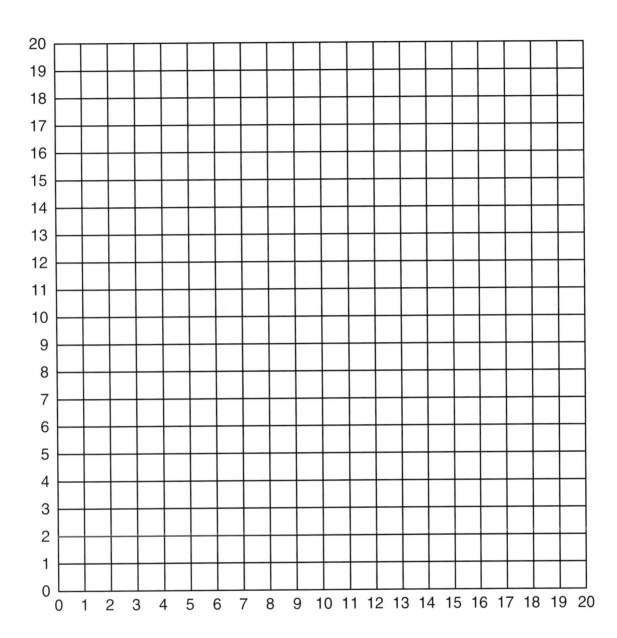

Seeing and Connecting Patterns across Representations

One of the most beautiful and amazing aspects of mathematics is the many different ways people can see mathematical ideas. When we value the multiple ways of seeing mathematical ideas, students are able to see mathematics as a creative and cool subject. One of my frustrations as a professor of mathematics education is the way students are introduced to algebra as a meaningless set of symbols, solving for x when they do not care or understand what x means. A much better way to introduce students to algebra is to give them patterns and encourage students to explore the different ways they see growth, using color, words, and, at some point, symbols. In this big idea, we have chosen to introduce students to the important mathematical idea of generalization, and to do so through having them visualize the growth of patterns. Students are often introduced to patterns in algebra classes, but instead of being asked to see the patterns in different ways, they are encouraged to count squares and then stare at tables of numbers to see whether they can work out generalizations. In our work with students, we give them patterns and ask them how they see growth; usually, rich conversations begin, with students sharing the different ways they visualize the growth. Giving students opportunity to color and represent the growth for others to see is powerful.

When students see growth visually and they are able to use words to describe it, they are connecting different pathways in the brain. When they use numbers, words, and visuals, more connections are made. The activities comprised in this big idea all give students opportunities to start generalizing, which is extremely valuable, and to express pattern growth in different ways and to connect across them.

In our Visualize activity, we ask students to study two patterns and to consider how they are growing. It is a good idea to ask them to find as many ways as they can, as this will encourage creativity. As they think about how patterns are growing, they are engaging in arguably the most central idea in algebra: generalizing. As they describe the growth using colors and words, different brain pathways will be activated, which is really good for their learning and understanding.

In our Play activity, students will be asked to create their own growing patterns using shapes and to analyze their patterns, making an activity for others to explore. When students are asked to create something for other students to work on, they are often excited and more interested, which deepens their learning. In this activity, the class will make a pattern carnival together and develop appreciation for mathematical patterns. They will be asked which patterns surprised or interested them, and this is an effective way of piquing their interest in and appreciation of mathematical patterns, which is an important goal in its own right.

In our Investigate activity, students will learn how to show a visual growing pattern in a table and on a coordinate graph. They will be encouraged to use different representations, such as a table, words, a graph, and a picture, and to connect between the different representations of the same idea, thus encouraging brain connections and conceptual understanding.

Jo Boaler

Two-Pattern Tango

Snapshot

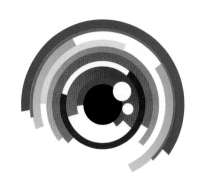

Students explore two similar visual growing patterns and develop ways of seeing and describing their growth. They compare the patterns and extend them to see how they diverge.

Connection to CCSS
5.OA.3

Agenda

Activity	Time	Description/Prompt	Materials
Launch	10 min	Introduce students to the two patterns and ask them to describe to a partner how they see growth across the patterns.	Two Patterns sheet, to display on projector
Explore	30+ min	Partners explore each pattern to find multiple ways to color-code and describe growth. Partners use their color-coding to compare the two patterns. Then students use their ideas to extend each pattern and find out what the 10th or 20th case would look like. Partners create a chart to show their findings.	• Pattern A sheet and Pattern B sheet, one or more per student • Grid paper (see appendix) • Colors • Chart and markers, for each partnership • Tape
Discuss	15+ min	Partners share their charts. Discuss the different ways students found to see and describe the growth of the two patterns, and discuss how the patterns compare. Examine how students have extended the patterns.	Students' charts
Extend	20+ min	Students develop ways to describe, for each pattern, how many squares will be in any case.	Make available: students' charts, additional pattern sheets, grid paper (see appendix), and colors

To the Teacher

Patterns are often presented numerically or symbolically to students, but we think visual patterns offer an important entry point to thinking abstractly about patterning. Students will be able to see the pattern before they are able to describe it. Pushing students to find multiple ways to describe the patterns through color coding and words helps them find interesting and productive ways to articulate what is happening in the pattern. They use these ways to springboard toward more abstract representations of patterns.

We have provided two patterns that look similar, but one is a linear pattern and the other is not. This central difference does not appear very significant in the early cases of the patterns, but quickly becomes quite large as students extend the pattern to the 10th case and beyond. We have not emphasized the use of numbers in this activity, focusing more on seeing and describing, but students will likely count squares and use the counts to help them think about the patterns. Moving between these representations—pictures, words, and numbers—is critical to making connections about patterning.

Activity

Launch

Launch the activity by showing students the Two Patterns sheet, as shown in Figure 5.1, on a projector. Tell students that each series, moving horizontally across the page, is a pattern. You might point out case 1, case 2, case 3, and case 4.

Ask students to look at the two patterns, one at a time. Ask, How do you see the pattern growing? Give students a few minutes to look and to turn and talk to a partner about how they see the growth of first one pattern and then the other. Often, at this point in a lesson, we ask students to share ideas, but in this lesson, we want to keep creativity open by not sharing yet. Tell students that the goal is to find diverse ways to describe and compare the growth of the two patterns. They will use their descriptions of the patterns to extend them.

Explore

Students work in partners, each with copies of the Pattern A and Pattern B sheets. Make available colors and grid paper (see appendix). Each student should keep their own record of their thinking on the pattern sheets, because students will see the patterns differently, and these differences will help them.

Students first work to figure out how to describe, using words and colors, how each pattern grows. The pattern sheets have several copies of each pattern on them so that students can push themselves to see in multiple ways how the pattern grows. Then students compare the two patterns: How are they growing differently? How are they growing similarly? Students use their colors, words, and numbers to support the comparison.

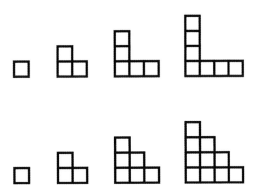

Figure 5.1 The Two Patterns

Challenge students to find ways to extend these patterns and find the 10th or 20th case of each pattern. Ask, How different will they be? Students may want to use grid paper (see appendix) as they extend the patterns.

Partners make a chart of what they've discovered, showing all the ways they have generated to see and describe the differences in the patterns as they continue to grow. Students may want to tape their pattern sheets to their charts and add labels and pattern extensions to show their thinking.

Discuss

Begin this discussion by having the different partnerships share the charts they have created to represent their thinking. You may want to have pairs take turns presenting their findings, or hold a gallery walk with all charts posted and students walking at their own pace from chart to chart.

As a class, discuss the following questions:

- What are the different ways we can see the growth of each pattern?
- What are the different ways we can describe the growth of each pattern?
- How do numbers help us compare? How do the visuals help us compare?
- What happens to each pattern as you extend it to the 10th or 20th case?

Extend

Challenge students to develop ways to use visuals, words, and numbers to describe, for each pattern, how many squares will be in any case. Students may need their charts, additional copies of the pattern sheets, grid paper (see appendix), and colors to tackle this extension.

Look-Fors

- **Are students finding multiple ways to see and describe each pattern?** We hope that working in partners, each student may see the pattern differently, which will help them generate even more ways to see the pattern. But if both partners see it the same way, they could become stuck seeing the pattern in the first way that came to them. You may want to ask the students to turn their paper to literally see the pattern from a different point of view, to help them find a new way of seeing. You might prompt them to examine the pattern from a different direction. For instance, if students see the staircase pattern as growing a new column to the left each time, you might ask them, What is happening to the bottom? Or along the stairs?

- **Are students counting?** Counting the squares will help students see and predict growth. It will also help them compare the two patterns. We have not directly asked students to count the squares, because we want to emphasize the visual and descriptive qualities of these patterns, but do notice when and how students are choosing to count. You may want to ask questions about how this will help them see their patterns and how they want to record their counts so that they don't forget what they have found.

- **How are students extending the patterns?** Students might extend the patterns by making each case. This will certainly work. However, encourage students to ask themselves, Do I need to make every case to know what the 10th or 20th will look like? Help students use their observations of the patterns to help them predict what those distant cases will look like. As they work to articulate what they know, they will be moving toward generalizing the patterns. Some students may skip directly to these distant cases, knowing exactly what they will look like. For these students, ask probing questions about how they know what to draw to support them in articulating the patterns they have in their minds.

Reflect

What were the most useful ways to see and describe the growth of the patterns? Why?

Two Patterns

Pattern A

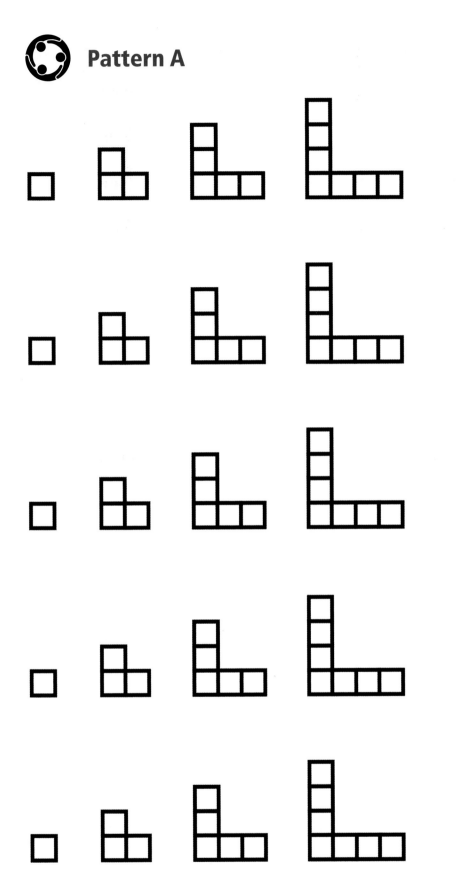

Pattern B

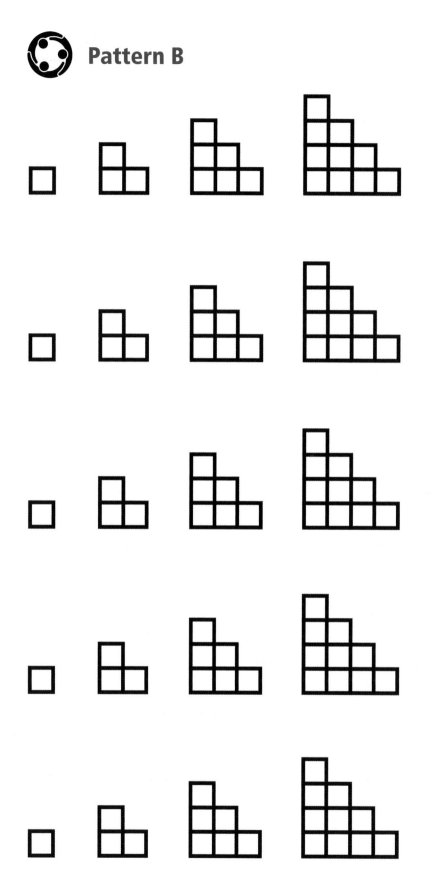

Pattern Carnival

Snapshot

Students create a pair of growing patterns using shapes, analyze their patterns, and then use them to create an activity for others to explore. Students' patterns become stations for a class pattern carnival.

Connection to CCSS
5.OA.3

Agenda

Activity	Time	Description/Prompt	Materials
Launch	10 min	Revisit how students saw and described pattern growth in the Visualize activity. Tell students that they will create two patterns of their own today, which they will put on a chart for a pattern carnival.	Examples of charts from the Visualize activity
Explore	40+ min	Partners create two similar patterns using shapes. They create a pattern record showing how the patterns grow, and analyze their similarities and differences through the 10th case. Then partners turn their patterns into charts with the first four cases of each pattern shown and some questions for others. These charts will be used in the pattern carnival.	• Chart and markers, for each partnership • Make available: pattern blocks, square tiles, grid paper (see appendix), and isometric dot paper (see appendix)
Launch	10 min	Discuss how the pattern carnival will work and the two roles students will play: station host and visitor.	

(Continued)

Activity	Time	Description/Prompt	Materials
Play	30 min	Stage the pattern carnival, with one partner hosting each pattern station and the other partners serving as visitors. Switch host and visitor roles halfway through the carnival. Hosts jot down interesting observations made by visitors, and visitors tackle the questions about the patterns at each station.	• Partners' pattern charts • Materials for the carnival stations, as needed: pattern blocks, square tiles, grid paper (see appendix), isometric dot paper (see appendix), and colors • Optional: sticky notes
Discuss	15 min	Discuss what students learned, as both hosts and visitors, about the patterns. Discuss interesting observations, comparisons, or questions.	

To the Teacher

This lesson builds directly on students' experiences in the Visualize activity. Encourage students to refer back to their work in that activity for ways to color-code, describe, and analyze patterns. In the first half of this lesson, students are asked to create and analyze a pair of patterns to create a pattern record. This can be done in a notebook or on a combination of grid, isometric dot (see appendix), and blank paper. Students can keep their pattern record with them during the carnival, if they want, to compare their own work to what others are doing with their patterns.

The pattern carnival is intended to extend across two or more days. The experience will be most interesting for all if students have adequate time to design, explore, analyze, and document their patterns. This may take one or more full class periods. Hosting the carnival could be on a separate day, and you may want to invite others, such as students from another class, to participate.

Activity

Launch

Launch by reminding students of the posters they made in the Visualize activity and how they described the growth of the two different patterns. Emphasize the ways they used colors, words, and numbers. Tell students that today they are going to create their own pair of patterns that are in some way similar to each other and in some way different. You may want to refer to the L-shaped pattern and the staircase pattern from the Visualize activity as an example of two patterns that are similar in some ways but also different. Figure 5.2 also shows two patterns that are similar but different. Tell students that they will analyze their patterns to describe how they grow, and create the patterns through the 10th case. They can use squares or other shapes to build their patterns.

Partners will create a chart that shows images of the first four cases of each pattern for a pattern carnival. Tell students that they will each get to host a station with their patterns, and everyone will get a chance to look at and investigate one another's patterns.

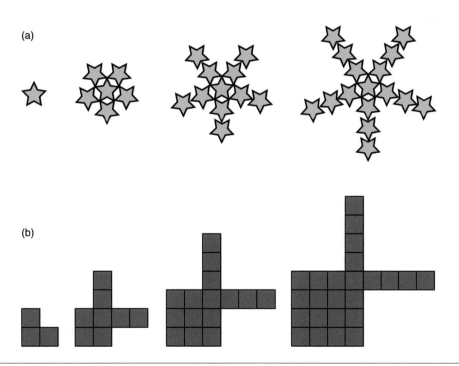

Figure 5.2 Two Different but Similar Growing Patterns Made with Shapes

Explore

Students work with a partner to design two similar but different growing patterns using shapes. Make available for students a variety of resources for creating and recording shape patterns, such as pattern blocks, square tiles, grid paper (see appendix), and isometric dot paper (see appendix). Each partnership will also need a chart and markers to construct their final carnival station.

Partners start by using materials to explore and design patterns. When they have two ideas they want to pursue, partners should create a pattern record to document how they see the two patterns. In the pattern record, students record the two patterns on grid or dot paper (see appendix), showing the patterns through at least the 10th case. Using words, numbers, and/or colors on their record of the patterns they've created, students also document how they see the patterns growing. Students should answer these questions: How do you see the similarities between the two patterns? How do you see the differences?

Once students have completed their pattern record, they turn their patterns into a chart for their carnival station. The chart should show just the first four cases of each pattern, as we did in the Visualize activity. Patterns should be clearly recorded so that others can look at them and think about how they see growth. Ask students to then add some questions for their classmates to consider as they look at the patterns, such as:

- How do you see the patterns growing?
- How are they similar? Different?
- What do you think the 10th [or 20th] case will look like?
- How many shapes will it take to build the 10th [or 20th] case of each pattern?

Students may want to stock their station with paper, colors, and/or manipulatives for visitors to use to explore the questions they've posed.

Launch

Gather students together to discuss the pattern carnival. Divide the partnerships in half so that one partner will host their group's station and the other will circulate to look at patterns. Midway through your carnival, these groups can swap roles so that all students get to host a station and visit stations. Discuss how to play each role in the carnival:

- Tell students that when they are hosting, they will display their chart with the first four cases of their two patterns. They will need to give visitors whatever tools they might need to investigate the patterns (for instance, grid or dot paper [see appendix], the right shapes). When students come to their station, hosts should invite them to investigate the patterns using the questions in the chart. Hosts jot down any ways that visitors see their patterns that are different, new, or interesting. You may want to give students sticky notes for this.
- Tell students that when they are visiting a station, they should be ready to investigate the patterns the hosts have made and try to answer the questions they have written. Encourage visitors to think about what makes the patterns interesting.

Have students set up their stations around the classroom.

Play

Run the carnival in two shifts so that everyone has a chance to host and visit. You will likely want to give students at least 15 minutes to serve in each role. Be sure to encourage station hosts to jot down notes about what their visitors do with their patterns that is different from how they themselves saw or thought about the patterns.

Discuss

Gather the students together to discuss the carnival. Ask the following questions:

- When people visited your station, did anyone see your patterns in a new way? What did they notice that you hadn't yet?
- When you were visiting stations, what did you see that interested or surprised you?
- What patterns prompted you to make interesting comparisons?
- What are you wondering about the patterns you made or saw?

Look-Fors

- **Are students creating patterns that they can continue predictably?** Students may construct designs, often with pattern blocks, that radiate from a central point or grow across a plane. They may be able to keep building these designs outward, but without a predictable pattern. Patterns have a structure to them, and students should be able to articulate the rule they are using to build their patterns from case to case. These rules need not be formally stated. They can simply be, for example, "I add one to each arm," or "I put a new layer on the outside." This kind of rule is the difference between a pattern and a design. Encourage students to talk about the rule and explain how they know what the next case will be. If they are working with a design instead of a pattern, encourage them to go back to the kernel of the design they started with and develop a rule they can use to build it out as a pattern.

- **Are students creating patterns that they themselves can analyze?** Students may make patterns so complex that they cannot yet articulate what is happening. This may simply be a matter of creating more cases, color-coding the pattern, and looking for ways to describe it, as we did in the Visualize activity. However, if students are stumped by their own patterns, others visiting their stations are likely to be, too. This may work well for a station; students could present their pattern as a genuine puzzle. You may also want to encourage students to create at least one pattern that they understand well to give them experience creating and analyzing visual patterns.

Reflect

What patterns did you see in the carnival that were most intriguing? Why?

Seeing Growth on a Graph
Snapshot

Students investigate how to show a visual growing pattern in a table and on a coordinate graph. Partners create their own patterns using pictures, tables, and graphs, and look for connections between these forms and among their patterns.

Connection to CCSS
5.G.1
5.G.2
5.OA.3

Agenda

Activity	Time	Description/Prompt	Materials
Launch	5–10 min	Show students the plus-sign pattern and ask them how they see the pattern growing. Ask students how they might use a table and a graph to show this pattern growing.	• Plus-Sign Pattern sheet, to display • Colors
Explore	20+ min	Partners investigate how to show the plus-sign pattern's growth on a table and a coordinate graph. They explore how growth appears in different ways in these three forms—pictures, table, and graph.	• Plus-Sign Pattern sheet, one per partnership • Plus-Sign Table and Graph Sheets, one per student • Optional: square tiles
Discuss	15 min	Discuss the ways students showed the pattern's growth visually, on the table, and on the coordinate graph, and what these three forms enable us to see about the pattern.	

(Continued)

Activity	Time	Description/Prompt	Materials
Explore	30+ min	Partners investigate how to create a growing pattern whose visual is different from the plus-sign pattern, but has the same table and graph. Partners investigate how to create a growing pattern with a different visual, table, and graph. Partners document both patterns.	• Square tiles • Grid paper (see appendix) • Growing Patterns Sheets, at least one per partnership
Discuss	20 min	Display and discuss the visual patterns students created that share a table and graph with the plus-sign pattern. Display and discuss the different patterns students constructed. Look for similarities, differences, and connections.	Students' patterns and space to display the two kinds of patterns created

To the Teacher

This investigation gives students the opportunity to take all the thinking they have been doing about visual patterns and see those patterns in new ways—on tables and in graphs. We have created a visual pattern for students to explore at the beginning of this investigation that is linear. The plus-sign pattern grows by four tiles in each case. This pattern should enable students to construct a table and a graph that show the growth in clear but different ways. The plus-sign pattern looks nothing like a line when shown as a group of tiles, and in the table, it appears as steadily increasing columns of odd numbers; but when plotted on the graph, the points become a crisp, clear line. These different ways of seeing the same pattern are at the heart of this investigation.

In the discussion for the first half of this investigation, we encourage you to introduce the idea of writing rules for patterns, or *generalizing*. As noted earlier, generalizing is a central practice in mathematics that students will continue to use throughout their lives, as they move from thinking about individual cases to identifying and describing the structures of patterns. Generalizing often involves writing equations to express rules, and the plus-sign pattern we offer here presents an opportunity for students to move toward this representation. The rules students write may involve numbers, operations, words, or even variables. It is not important for students to use algebra to generalize, but if they are interested in doing so, this is an appropriate activity to develop that idea. Critically, students should only move to an algebraic expression from a visual understanding of growth.

In the second half of the investigation, students are asked to make two kinds of patterns: one with a different visual but with the same table and graph as the plus-sign pattern, and one that is completely different. Each of these presents its own challenge. Reimagining the plus-sign visual means maintaining the numerical pattern while thinking differently about the arrangement of squares. Creating an entirely new pattern may lead students toward nonlinear graphs. The patterns students create may be challenging to generalize, depending on what they design. Encourage students to try to generalize in whatever ways make sense to them. Embrace all of these challenges, and be sure to include in your class discussions what made these hard and what surprising things students discovered.

Activity

Launch

Building on the pattern carnival, launch this lesson by showing students a new pattern, the plus-sign pattern, on a projector. Ask students to turn and talk to a partner about how they see the pattern growing. Take some student ideas and color-code the pattern to show different ways it grows. You may want to have multiple copies of the Plus-Sign Pattern sheet available to make your color coding clear. Tell students that these are all ways that we can see the pattern growing using the shapes, and that today we are going to investigate new ways of seeing growth. Ask students, How could we use a table and a graph to help us see the growth in new ways?

Explore

Students work in partners to investigate how to show the growth of the plus-sign pattern on a table and on a graph. Provide students with a copy of the Plus-Sign Pattern sheet and copies of the Plus-Sign Table and Graph Sheet, one per student. Students may also want square tiles to extend the pattern.

After students have figured out ways to show the pattern on the table and graph, ask them: How do you see the growth on the table and the graph? How does the growth of the pattern look different in the picture, table, and graph?

Discuss

Gather students together with their Plus-Sign Table and Graph Sheets to discuss the following questions:

- How did you show the pattern's growth on the table? How did you show the growth on the graph?
- How do you see the growth on the table and the graph?
- How can we use the graph and table to describe the growth?
- How does growth look different in the picture, table, and graph?
- How do the table and graph change what you see? What might they be useful for?

Explore

Partners work together to create (at least) two new patterns using squares:

- One pattern should look different than our plus-sign pattern but have the same table and graph.
- (At least) one pattern should have a different table and graph.

For each pattern, partners create at least the first six cases of the pattern visually, using square tiles and grid paper (see appendix) to document the patterns. For each pattern that has a table and graph different from those of the plus-sign pattern, partners create a table and graph to show their pattern's growth on a Growing Patterns Sheet. Ask partners to record, How would you describe the growth of each pattern?

You might encourage students to think about generalizing their patterns, in whatever ways they can. Keep in mind that some patterns students create may be nonlinear and difficult for them to generalize formally at this point. If it surfaces, this observation—that some patterns are easier than others to generalize—would be a useful topic to return to in the discussion.

Discuss

Gather students together and display all patterns that have the same table and graph as the plus-sign pattern. Compare the different patterns by discussing the following questions:

- What do these patterns have in common?
- Do you think there are others possible?
- What was hard about making these patterns match the graph?
- How did you figure out how to do it?

Display all the patterns that have tables and graphs that are different from those of the plus-sign pattern.

- What do the different patterns have in common?
- What makes them different?
- How could we group them to show what they have in common?
- What connections do you see?
- What questions do you have about these patterns? What are you wondering?

If students worked on generalizing their patterns, you might ask them to share the rules they created or the challenges they faced when trying to write a rule.

Look-Fors

- **How are students moving between the forms of representation?** Moving between pictures, numbers, tables, and graphs is complex—and new—work for students. Encourage students to slow down and think through the connection between specific pictures, numbers, rows on the table, and points on the graph. Ask, Are these showing the same information? How are they related? Students will find different pathways crossing back and forth between forms. Some will want to complete the table fully, then complete the graph fully. Others may work best by working across forms for each point. Ask students if the way they are working is helping them make sense and keep track of the different relationships and values.

- **Are students creating a pattern that matches the table and graph of the plus-sign pattern?** For this part of the investigation, the challenge to students is to find a new visual pattern that could have the same table and graph as the plus-sign pattern. Students will need to think about how each case grows numerically and reimagine a visual pattern that grows in this way. Student may find an entry point with square tiles, which they can count out for each case and then rearrange to find new visual patterns, while not changing the number of tiles used.

- **Are students making connections between the different forms of pattern representation?** As students work to represent patterns in pictures, numbers, tables, and graphs, it is important to continue to emphasize that these are the *same* pattern. Different ways of showing the pattern offer us different ways to understand the pattern and how it grows. You may want to ask students as they work, or ask the whole class in the discussion, to focus in on parts of a pattern (such as adding a tile to each arm of the plus sign in each case) and ask, How do we see this part of the pattern in the picture, the table, and the graph?

Reflect

What different things can you learn about a pattern by looking at a picture, at a table, or at a graph? Which do you think gives the most information? Why?

Plus-Sign Pattern

How do you see the pattern growing?

Plus-Sign Table and Graph Sheet

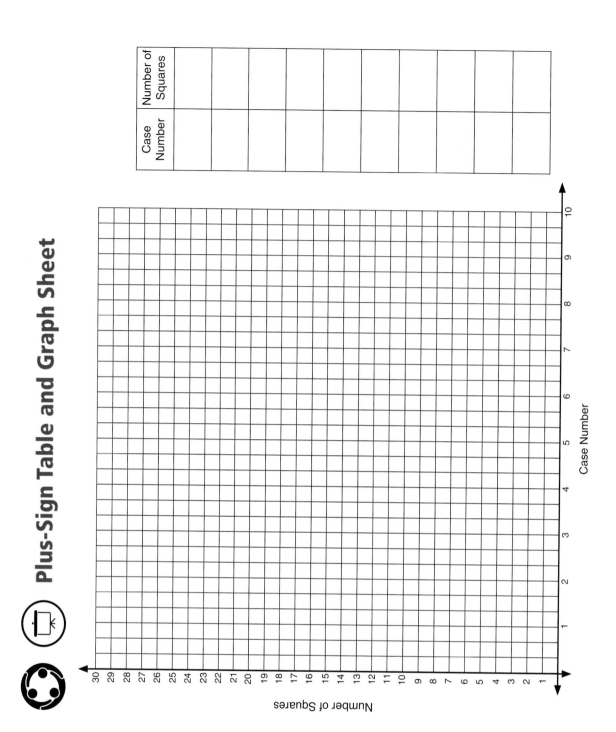

Case Number	Number of Squares

Growing Patterns Sheet

Case Number	Number of Squares

Number of Squares

Case Number

Understanding Fraction Multiplication Visually

Tiling with Wholes and Pieces

Many students learn to multiply fractions using a rule or algorithm, but lack any understanding of how they have arrived at their answer or what their answer represents. I have encountered a lot of students who have been able to multiply fractions and get an answer, but have no idea what it means. This lack of awareness makes their future understanding fragile. Further, if students have learned to multiply fractions only by multiplying numerators and multiplying denominators, they may get correct answers, but then go on to make errors when adding and subtracting fractions. It is very important in all mathematics for students to work with meaning, understanding what they are doing and what is happening. In 2009, the question in Figure 6.1 was offered on the NAEP tests.

The correct answer is A, but only 55% of fourth graders chose this response. This suggests that many students had not learned to *see* fraction equivalence. In the activities that make up this big idea, we give students many opportunities to think about fraction multiplication visually. The advantage of this approach is that students actually see what takes place when two fractions are multiplied, which enables them to understand what is happening to the size of the fractions when they multiply them together. In the different activities of this big idea, we give students

Which picture shows that $\frac{3}{4}$ is the same as $\frac{6}{8}$?

(From 2009 NAEP Assessment for 4th Graders)

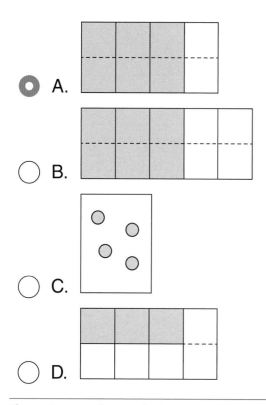

A.

B.

C.

D.

Figure 6.1 Fraction Equivalence Question

opportunities to multiply fractions by fractions, and fractions by whole numbers visually. As they see visuals and numbers they will again be creating opportunities for important brain connections.

In our Visualize activity, we ask students to work with a visual of a pan of brownies and think about how much is left if a fraction of a fraction is eaten. It is intentional that we ask students to produce visual proofs for one another, so even if they work out an answer numerically, they need to show a visual proof. The goal of the activity is for students to develop area models for fraction multiplication. This is not something you need to show the students, and in fact it is better to let them come up with their own visuals, as this will give you insights into the students' understanding and give them more opportunities to build brain connections. We also ask students to construct tables of results, which will help them connect the numbers with the visual proofs.

In our Play activity, students will use the sheet of number visuals that we introduced on youcubed.org a few years ago. This incredibly generative sheet shows numbers drawn as factors, and if students have not encountered it before, it is best to ask students to write the numbers that go with each visual and spend time looking for patterns in the sheet. They will start to see many different patterns and develop a greater appreciation for the ways numbers are constructed. In our activity, we ask students to find numbers where $\frac{1}{2}$, $\frac{1}{3}$, and $\frac{1}{4}$ of the number result in a whole-number answer. This should be puzzling for students and may create opportunities for you to tell them how important struggle is for the brain, and that when they are making mistakes and struggling, these are the best times for brain growth.

In our Investigate activity, students are given another puzzle:

I have four different numbers. When I take $\frac{1}{2}$ of one number, $\frac{1}{3}$ of another number, $\frac{1}{4}$ of another, and $\frac{1}{5}$ of the last number and add them together, I get a sum of 20. What could my four numbers be?

It is important in this activity that students record their thinking carefully, in pictures, numbers, and/or words. The students will be working with four numbers simultaneously, so a system of recording will really help their thinking. This activity could be a good opportunity to show the students what can be gained by careful recording. As is the case when teaching any ideas, students often learn them more effectively if they come up in the context of a problem they are working with, rather than being told the ideas before they start.

Jo Boaler

Fractions in a Pan

Snapshot

Students begin to explore fraction multiplication using area models of a brownie pan. Students look for patterns in their solutions and connect these patterns to multiplication.

> Connection to CCSS
> 5.NF.4
> 5.NF.6

Agenda

Activity	Time	Description/Prompt	Materials
Launch	10 min	Tell students that you (or someone else) made a pan of brownies and ate $\frac{1}{3}$ of the pan, leaving $\frac{2}{3}$ left over. Pose the question, If someone eats $\frac{1}{4}$ of the leftovers, what fraction *of the whole pan* will that person eat?	Optional: individual whiteboards and markers for partners
Explore	20+ min	Partners work to construct visual proofs of the brownie pan problem that they can use to solve and to convince others of their solution.	Make available: copies of the Brownie Pan Template, blank paper, brown construction paper, scissors, and colors
Discuss	15+ min	Discuss and chart the different visual proofs students have created to solve this problem. Compare the different proofs. Start a second chart with a table for recording students' solutions for this problem and the next. Introduce the second activity.	Charts and markers Optional: tape
Explore	20+ min	Partners again work to construct convincing visual proofs. Given a pan of brownies with $\frac{2}{3}$ of the brownies left over, students choose a fraction of the leftovers someone could eat. They then figure out what fraction of the whole pan would be eaten.	• Brownie Pan Template • Make available: blank paper, brown construction paper, scissors, and colors

Discuss	15+ min	Students share the different fractions they selected, the model they created, and the solutions they found. Record these different fractions and solutions in the class table. Discuss the patterns students notice and connect these to multiplication.	Chart with table, and markers

To the Teacher

We have selected pans of brownies as the context for this task to encourage students to develop area models for the multiplication of fractions. Just as arrays can support students in thinking visually about decomposing whole numbers for multiplication, rectangular area models can be used for fraction multiplication. These fraction multiplication area models can emerge from opportunities to cut wholes, such as a pan of brownies, vertically and horizontally, shading the fractions created by these cuts. The model in Figure 6.2 is an example of making the cuts in this activity. In the figure, you can see first cutting the pan into thirds and shading the $\frac{2}{3}$ that remain. Then by cutting the pan again, this time into fourths, and shading the $\frac{1}{4}$ that will be eaten, the entire pan is portioned into equal-size pieces, and the portion eaten—the product of $\frac{2}{3}$ and $\frac{1}{4}$—can be seen easily as $\frac{2}{12}$.

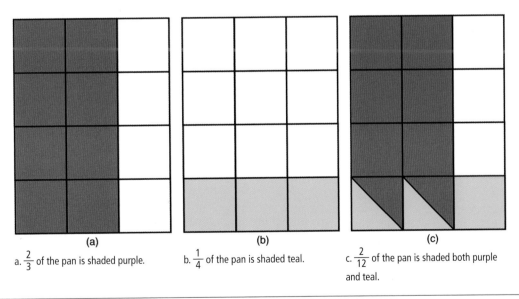

(a)

a. $\frac{2}{3}$ of the pan is shaded purple.

(b)

b. $\frac{1}{4}$ of the pan is shaded teal.

(c)

c. $\frac{2}{12}$ of the pan is shaded both purple and teal.

Figure 6.2 Area Model Fraction Multiplication

The goal of this activity is for students to develop area models, like the one shown, for fraction multiplication. You do not need to model this method; instead we want students to create it themselves. In the discussion, highlight the models students invent that support seeing $\frac{2}{12}$ clearly.

Activity

Launch

Tell students that you (or someone else) made a pan of brownies for dessert and that your (or their) family (or friends) ate a third of the pan, so there is $\frac{2}{3}$ of the pan left over. Ask students to turn and talk to a partner about this question: What do you imagine the pan of brownies looks like now? If students have individual whiteboards, you could ask them to draw what they imagine. Ask students to share what they think the brownie pan could look like now. Use this as an opportunity to assess student understanding and clarify ways to represent the brownie pan that make sense. You might record on the board or on a chart some examples students came up with. For instance, students might cut the pan vertically or horizontally into three equal parts. Be sure students are constructing rectangular models by clarifying that your brownie pan is a rectangle, if necessary. Some students might ask whether the brownies are precut into individual pieces. Tell students that what remains in the pan is just one large, uncut brownie.

When the class has clarity about what the pan might look like, tell students that tonight for dessert someone is going to eat $\frac{1}{4}$ of what is left over. Ask, What fraction *of the pan* will that person be eating? Emphasize that the pan is the unit, or the whole, and be sure students understand that the person will be eating $\frac{1}{4}$ of what remains in the pan, but that you want to know what fraction of the whole pan this will be.

Explore

Partners work to answer these questions: What fraction *of the pan* will the person be eating? How will you show or draw this situation? Students can use whatever materials they choose to model to find solutions and make visual proofs. They might want to use the Brownie Pan Template, draw their own rectangles, or fold paper. Some students may find brown construction paper particularly useful for modeling the brownie pan. Encourage students to create a model that they can explain so others will be convinced of their solution.

Discuss

Gather students to share strategies and their visual proofs. Make a chart to show the different ways that students have solved this problem. You may want to tape students' work to the chart to show their different models. Discuss the following questions:

- What fraction of the pan will the person get to eat?
- How can we tell using your visual proof?
- What do the different models have in common?

In your discussion, be sure that students come to consensus on a solution and the models that make sense. You might ask students which of the visual proofs they find the most convincing or which makes the most sense to them right now, and have them explain why.

Start a second chart that contains a table with the column headings illustrated. Fill in the table for this first problem, using whatever fractions students came up with for the solution:

Fraction of the Pan Left Over	Fraction of the Brownies Eaten Tonight	Fraction of the Pan Eaten Tonight
$\frac{2}{3}$	$\frac{1}{4}$	$\frac{2}{12} = \frac{1}{6}$

Then introduce the second part of this activity. Draw another brownie pan on the board or on a chart, showing $\frac{2}{3}$ of the brownies left over, just as at the start of the first problem. Then pose the task, reminding students that they are in charge of choosing, with their partner, what fraction of the pan someone might eat. It could be a lot or very little.

Explore

Students return to their partnerships to explore this task. Given a brownie pan with $\frac{2}{3}$ of the brownies left over, what fraction of the leftover brownies *could* someone eat? What fraction *of the whole pan* would that person be eating? Students get to choose the fractions they want to work with and create visual proofs for the fractions eaten. Students can use the same kind of visual proof they constructed in the first task, or try a different way, perhaps something they saw another pair share in the discussion. Encourage students to try several different fractions and to make clear proofs for each.

Discuss

Gather students together to share the different fractions they chose and the fraction of the brownie pan that would be eaten. Fill in these findings on the table and ask students to share their visual proofs. Be sure students are presenting convincing proofs, and be sure to ask the class whether they are convinced by the evidence shared.

After several pairs have had a chance to share, ask the class to look at the table you've made together. Ask students, What patterns do you see? You may want to have students turn and talk to a partner to give them time to notice and think. In your discussion of patterns, support students in looking across the rows and attending to the relationship between the fractions in each way of cutting the brownies. Students may notice that the answer is the product of the numerators over the product of the denominators. So that this doesn't simply become a trick, ask students why this pattern makes sense with the models they have constructed. Ask, Where is the multiplication? If students readily see these patterns, take this opportunity to name that what they were doing was *multiplying* the two fractions, so that $\frac{2}{3} \times \frac{1}{4} = \frac{2}{12}$.

Look-Fors

- **Are students clear about what each fraction represents?** Multiplication of fractions can be confusing because the unit changes within the problem. For instance, $\frac{2}{3}$ is the fraction *of the pan*, $\frac{1}{4}$ is the fraction *of the leftovers* (or of $\frac{2}{3}$), and the solution $\frac{2}{12}$. is the fraction *of the pan.* Support students in talking clearly about what each fraction represents, using the units, to maintain sense making.

- **Are students cutting the pan into equal-size pieces?** Some students may draw lines on their models—cut—only the portion of the brownies that remain. This leads to regions in the pan that are different sizes, making it hard to see the fraction *of the pan* that is being eaten. Point out that their regions are different sizes and ask whether there is a way to cut so that there will be equal-size pieces. Some students may find this easier to do with paper folding than with drawing.

- **Are students noticing the multiplicative relationship between the fractions?** One goal of this lesson is to support students in connecting the visual models to multiplication. When you have students examine patterns in the class table, students may see this relationship. And when they do, you should name what students have been doing as multiplication and show a number sentence that could be used to represent the problems. However, if students do not yet see this pattern, you may want to give them more time to work on generating examples for the table, or send them back to work with their partner to look for patterns, before telling students that this is multiplication.

Reflect

How are the brownie pans connected to multiplication? Use an example or draw a picture to make your thinking clear.

Brownie Pan Template

Pieces and Parts

Snapshot

In this activity, we open the door to thinking about multiplying a fraction by a whole number using the number visuals to support students in solving a fraction puzzle.

Connection to CCSS
5.NF.4

Agenda

Activity	Time	Description/Prompt	Materials
Launch	10–15 min	Show students the Number Visuals Sheet and talk about the numbers represented and the patterns students notice. Introduce using the visuals to think about fractions by asking students to look for numbers they can see $\frac{1}{4}$ of. Pose today's task and clarify the constraints.	• Number Visuals Sheet, for display • Colors • Optional: Number Visuals Sheet, one per student or pair
Play	30+ min	Partners use the Number Visuals Sheet to identify numbers where $\frac{1}{2}$, $\frac{1}{3}$, and $\frac{1}{4}$ of the number results in a whole-number answer. Students might also look for a number not shown on the Number Visuals Sheet that meets these constraints.	• Number Visuals Sheet, multiple copies per pair • Colors
Discuss	15–20 min	Discuss the strategies students developed for finding numbers that meet the constraints. Look for patterns in the solutions students identified, and consider how those patterns help students think about other numbers that might satisfy the constraints.	• Chart and markers • Number Visuals Sheets, to show and mark up • Colors
Extend	30+ min	Choose two or three new unit fractions to serve as constraints, and use the Number Visuals Sheets to find solutions for these fractions.	• Number Visuals Sheet, multiple copies per pair • Colors

To the Teacher

The goal of this activity is to give students a visual experience of multiplying a fraction by a whole number before we name this as fraction multiplication. Here students just think about finding a fraction *of* a whole number. Later we can substitute a multiplication symbol for the word *of,* and students will then have two equivalent and useful ways of thinking about multiplication: $\frac{1}{3} \times 18$ is the same as $\frac{1}{3}$ of 18. We encourage you to take advantage of the many connections students are likely to make as they use the Number Visuals Sheet to explore the puzzle. Students may implicitly move between thinking of finding, say, $\frac{1}{4}$ of 20 and dividing 20 by 4 to get 5. Students may think about finding numbers that work with $\frac{1}{3}$ by counting by 3s or naming the multiples of 3 (that is, 3, 6, 9, 12, 15, 18, . . .). Students might say that all the even numbers work with $\frac{1}{2}$. In each of these cases, students are making connections between finding a fraction of a whole number, factors, multiples, properties of numbers, multiplication, and division. These are useful connections that can make students' thinking more flexible and grounded in sense making, rather than procedures. We encourage you to notice these aloud for students as they occur and ask whether these connections are always, or only sometimes, true. For instance, you might ask: Are you saying that can you find $\frac{1}{3}$ of *all* the multiples of 3? Why?

Activity

Launch

Launch the lesson by showing the Number Visuals Sheet on a projector. If students have never seen the number visuals, give them a few minutes to look for patterns. Have students turn and talk to a partner about what they notice. You may want to hand out a copy so that students can see them up close as they talk to a partner. If students are familiar with the number visuals, you might ask them what they remember about these numbers or how they have used this representation in the past.

Ask students to share the patterns they notice or remember. If no one points out what numbers are represented, ask students what numbers each picture shows. Record the number for each visual representation on your class sheet so that students can see the structure. Record any other patterns students notice. We encourage you to use different colors to show the different patterns students see.

Tell students that these representations can be used to explore whole numbers, as they may have in the past, but today they are going to use them to explore fractions. Ask students to look at the number visuals again, and ask, If we want a whole-number answer, which numbers on this page can you find $\frac{1}{4}$ of? Give students a minute to turn and talk, then take some suggestions, along with students' reasoning. Be sure to draw students' attention to the ways they can use the number visuals as evidence, and mark up the Number Visuals Sheet to show how students saw $\frac{1}{4}$.

Pose the puzzle. Be sure to make clear that students are looking for numbers where they can find $\frac{1}{2}$ of the number, $\frac{1}{3}$ of the number, and $\frac{1}{4}$ of the number and get a whole-number answer each time.

Play

Students work in partners with copies of the Number Visuals Sheet to mark up with colors, if they choose. Partners explore the following puzzles:

- Can you find a number represented on this page where $\frac{1}{2}$, $\frac{1}{3}$, and $\frac{1}{4}$ of the number results in a whole number? Which numbers can you find that satisfy these conditions?
- What numbers not pictured on this page satisfy these conditions? How might you draw them? How could you use your visuals to prove that they satisfy the conditions?

Students may want to play with each fraction separately at first, using a Number Visuals Sheet to identify numbers that they can find $\frac{1}{2}$ of, then a separate sheet to identify numbers they can find $\frac{1}{3}$ of, and so forth. Students could then look across their different sheets to see what numbers the sheets have in common. Alternatively, students might decide to search number by number. For instance, they might start with the number 1 and ask themselves: Can I find $\frac{1}{2}$ of it? Can I find $\frac{1}{3}$ of it? Can I find $\frac{1}{4}$ of it? This strategy enables students to eliminate numbers or find solutions, one by one. These are just two approaches students might use, and there are certainly others. Encourage students to develop their own process and to think about how to be systematic.

Discuss

Gather students together, with their Number Visuals Sheets, and discuss the following questions:

- What strategies did you use to find a number where $\frac{1}{2}$, $\frac{1}{3}$, and $\frac{1}{4}$ of it is a whole number?
- How could we use the visuals to prove that these numbers satisfy these conditions?
- What patterns do you notice in the numbers that satisfy the conditions?
- What numbers not pictured could also satisfy these conditions? How do you know? How do the patterns in our solutions help us predict larger number solutions? How could they be drawn?

Use blank copies of the Number Visuals Sheet and chart paper to record students' strategies for identifying solutions and eliminating numbers that do not work. As students are sharing their thinking, ask students to say not just which numbers have a whole-number solution but what that solution is. For instance, students might say that you can find $\frac{1}{2}$ of 14. Follow up by asking, What is $\frac{1}{2}$ of 14? Record this on your chart or Number Visuals Sheet as part of the evidence: $\frac{1}{2}$ of 14 is 7. Recording in this way will support students in seeing number patterns and connecting those to the visual patterns on the sheet.

Extend

Choose a different set of two or three unit fractions and see what numbers students can find that satisfy these conditions. You could have students select the two or three unit fractions with a partner, have the class choose them together, or you might choose them yourself. Keep in mind that some combinations of unit fractions, such as $\frac{1}{10}$, $\frac{1}{4}$, and $\frac{1}{8}$, will lead to no solutions on the Number Visuals Sheet. This could be interesting itself, leading to the question, Does this mean there are no numbers that satisfy these conditions? For some students, however, this might be quite frustrating. Some interesting combinations could be: $\frac{1}{3}$, $\frac{1}{5}$, and $\frac{1}{10}$, or $\frac{1}{2}$ and $\frac{1}{7}$.

Look-Fors

- **Are students connecting fractions and factors?** The numbers students can find $\frac{1}{2}$ of are also numbers that have 2 as a factor, and are even numbers. Connecting these mathematical ideas is a key outcome. It also makes sense to think of multiplying by $\frac{1}{2}$ as the same as dividing by 2. As students play with the number visuals, highlight places where students are moving across these different ideas and making connections between fractions, multiplication, division, factors, multiples, and number properties. You might want to bring these observations to the class discussion and have students debate whether they are always true. For instance, you might say that one partnership had the idea that all the numbers that you could find $\frac{1}{2}$ of were even numbers, and ask whether students agree or disagree with this and why. You might chart these different connection and observations and ask students to see whether they can find any counterexamples.

- **Are students thinking systematically?** Some students might start with a hunch and explore it first. For instance, a partnership might think that 12 is a flexible number and that maybe it will be a solution. This is fine as a starting place. But as students move into playing with the different fractions and number visuals, they will need a system if they hope to find all the numbers that satisfy the conditions of the problem. Ask students how they will know which numbers work and which ones don't. You also might probe the hunches that they started with, as they might be built on some useful assumptions. For instance, the notion that 12 is flexible is useful, and it is flexible because of its many factors. If students can articulate this, then that could lead to quickly testing and eliminating many other numbers, such as the primes.

- **How are students organizing their work to see useful patterns?** Juggling three fractions and 35 number visuals on multiple pieces of paper can be an organizational challenge. Support students in thinking about how they will keep track of what they notice so that they can use those observations to hunt for solutions. You could ask: Will color help? What labels could be useful? What is the job of each piece of paper? How are you recording what works and what doesn't?

Reflect

What does it mean to find $\frac{1}{5}$ (or $\frac{1}{3}$ or $\frac{1}{4}$) of a number? Use examples or drawings to help you explain.

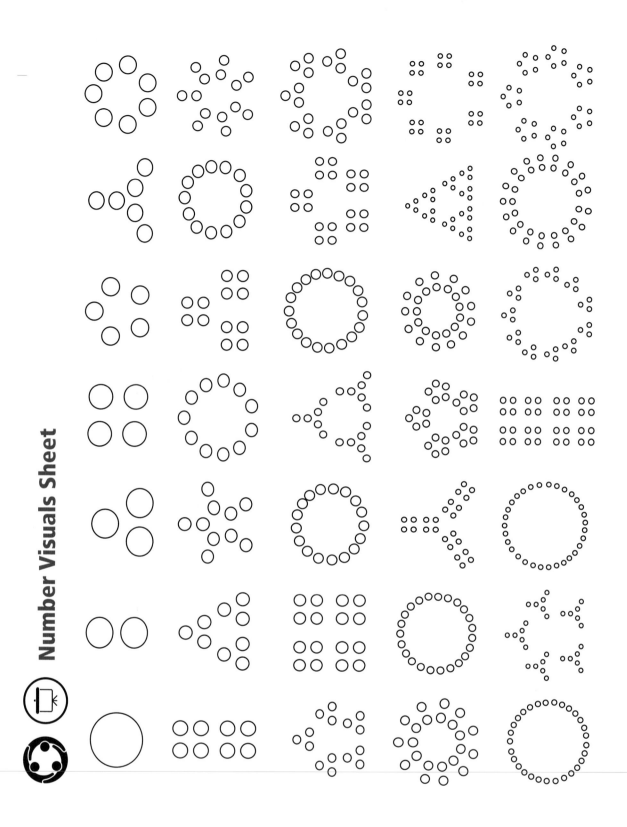

Number Visuals Sheet

The Sum of the Parts

Snapshot

We extend students' work with finding a fraction of a whole number to investigate and create visual proofs for fraction puzzles. We name finding a fraction *of* a whole number as multiplication.

Connection to CCSS 5.NF.4 5.OA.1	

Agenda

Activity	Time	Description/Prompt	Materials
Launch	5–10 min	Remind students of their previous fraction work with the Number Visuals Sheet. Pose the puzzle and make sure the constraints are clear. Ask students to solve and present evidence of their solutions in as many ways as possible.	Number Visuals Sheet (from Play activity), to show on projector
Explore	30+ min	Partners work to solve the puzzle: I have four different numbers. When I take $\frac{1}{2}$ of one number, $\frac{1}{3}$ of another number, $\frac{1}{4}$ of another, and $\frac{1}{5}$ of the last number and add them together, I get a sum of 20. What could my four numbers be? Students record evidence of their solutions using pictures, numbers, and/or words.	• Make available: multiple Number Visuals Sheets per partnership • Multiple Number Visual Card decks per partnership • Scissors • Colors
Discuss	20+ min	Discuss students' solutions and their evidence. Name their work as multiplication and model ways of rewriting solutions with number sentences. Determine a way to organize the solutions and look for patterns.	• Chart and markers • Optional: other tools for organizing solutions, such as paper and bulletin board
Extend	30+ min	Modify the task to build on areas of student interest, by changing the sum or the number of values or by asking students to write their own puzzles.	Make available: Number Visuals Sheet and colors

To the Teacher

This investigation names one big idea—multiplication of a fraction by a whole number—and introduces a second, the use of grouping symbols. Although students will have already played with the notion of finding a fraction of a whole number, in this lesson we formalize this operation as multiplication and share with students conventional ways of recording this work. If students do not yet have experience with grouping symbols, you do not need to explain all the details of their use. It is enough to show how these symbols group together the different parts of the problem and make it easier to see the components of the solution. Often the introduction of new symbols leads to students' trying them out in lots of situations, sometimes conventionally and sometimes not. This lesson is a good opportunity for students to try out parentheses without yet needing to fully and accurately reflect the order of operations.

As students investigate, they may look for ways to solve the problem more efficiently. Students might systematically search for all the numbers that they can find $\frac{1}{2}$ of, or $\frac{1}{4}$ of, and so on. They may record these possibilities in a table, list, or stack of Number Visual Cards. In this way, students may be creating a menu of options they can use to find multiple solutions. This kind of searching for patterns should be embraced. In order to keep students making sense, they still need to find visual proof for each solution, which confirms what they found using numbers.

Activity

Launch

Launch this lesson by reminding students of the number visuals they used in the Play activity by displaying the Number Visuals Sheet on a projector. You may want to revisit the charts you created finding fractions of the visuals, reminding students of the patterns or connections they noticed. Tell students that today we are going to continue to think about finding a fraction *of* a whole number. Then pose the puzzle for this investigation. Make sure the constraints of the problem are clear before you send students off to work. Tell students that you'd like them to find as many different ways to solve the problem as they can, and for each solution, they need to record evidence. Their evidence might include a combination of pictures, numbers, and words.

Explore

Students work in partners to investigate the following problem:

- I have four different numbers. When I take $\frac{1}{2}$ of one number, $\frac{1}{3}$ of another number, $\frac{1}{4}$ of another, and $\frac{1}{5}$ of the last number and add them together, I get a sum of 20. What could my four numbers be?
- Find as many different ways as you can to solve this problem. For each solution you find, show a visual proof, with labels, on the Number Visuals Sheet.

Make available to students Number Visuals Sheets, decks of Number Visual Cards, scissors, and colors to support their thinking. Some students may want to use the card decks to create a stack of numbers they can find $\frac{1}{2}$ of, $\frac{1}{3}$ of, $\frac{1}{4}$ of, or $\frac{1}{5}$ of. Alternatively, students may use them as a bridge to writing expressions, by laying out the parts of their solution visually. They are free to use numbers not shown on the Number Visuals Sheet, but they should draw any larger numbers as part of their evidence. See Figure 6.3 for an example.

Discuss

Gather students together with their evidence to discuss the following questions. Chart students' thinking and examples of their evidence:

- What solutions did you find?
- How did you use what you found to help you find new solutions?

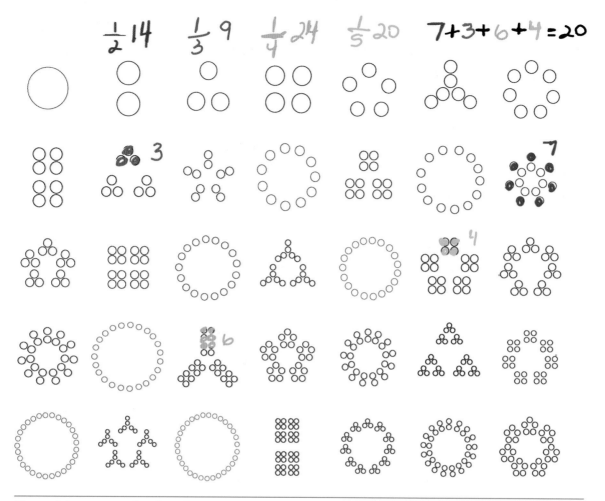

Figure 6.3 An Example of Student Work Showing a Solution

Show students how to turn their findings into number sentences by naming what they have been doing as *multiplication*. For instance, tell them that "$\frac{1}{5}$ of 20 is 4" the same thing as $\frac{1}{5} \times 20 = 4$. Ask students to help you rewrite some of the parts of a solution as multiplication number sentences. You may want to combine these individual number sentences into a single equation using parentheses to show the entire solution, such as $(\frac{1}{2} \times 10) + (\frac{1}{3} \times 24) + (\frac{1}{4} \times 12) + (\frac{1}{5} \times 20) = 20$.

Then ask students to look back over all the solutions they have come up with as a class. Ask students, Is there a way to organize these solutions to look for patterns? Give students a moment to turn and talk to a partner about ideas. Discuss ideas for how to organize solutions. Students may suggest some kind of table or rewriting all of the solutions using equations. Students might suggest writing each solution on a piece of paper or index card and organizing them on a bulletin board in some way.

Come to agreement about some way to organize and display all the solutions so that you can look for patterns, then implement your plan. Looking at your organized solutions, discuss the following questions:

- What do you notice about our solutions?
- Which numbers did we all use the most often? Why?
- What numbers did not get used? Why?
- How would you use these patterns to search for other solutions?

If students are interested, you might ask them to go back and search for additional solutions using their observations from the discussion.

Extend

Modify the task to build on areas of student interest. Ask that students work to write their solutions in number sentences. You might ask the following:

- What set of four numbers satisfy the conditions if the sum is 30 [or another number students select]?
- What if you have five numbers and you extend the task to include $\frac{1}{6}$ of a number, and the sum of the five numbers remains 20?
- Choose your own list of four unit fractions. What solutions can you find using these four unit fractions, where the sum of the products is 20?

Or ask students to write and try to solve their own puzzles. They might find problems that have no solution, one solution, or several solutions. All are interesting to investigate and prove.

Look-Fors

- **How are students organizing the components of their solutions to keep track?** This investigation asks students to juggle four fractions of four whole numbers with a maximum sum. With so many parts, students will need systems for organizing the pieces they are collecting and using toward a complete solution. If you notice students with lots of parts getting somewhat lost in their own work, ask: What parts have you figured out? How can you record or organize those parts so you can see what you have or what you still have left to find? Students may want to use the Number Visuals Sheets, one per solution, as a way of organizing. Labels often help keep track of the values, such as recording $\frac{1}{2}$ of 14 as 7.

- **Are students using one solution to help them find new ones?** Rather than starting over each time, students can modify one solution repeatedly to generate new ones. Some students might like to put each component on a sticky note so that they can rearrange them to make new solutions, such as pulling out $\frac{1}{2}$ of 14 = 7 and substituting $\frac{1}{2}$ of 10 = 5 for a new solution. This kind of thinking focuses on patterning and the underlying structure of the problem.

- **How are students reasoning about finding a fraction of a whole number?** Students may connect this work to multiplication or division of whole numbers, or to the work done in the Play activity. Students may benefit from using the Number Visuals Sheet again to better see and justify their thinking.

- **How are students translating their work into number sentences?** At the end of the lesson, you will give students the opportunity to reframe their work as multiplication of fractions by a whole number. You may also introduce grouping symbols. Pay attention to how students are connecting the meaning of these symbols to their own work. The symbols should serve as a new way to label their existing thinking. Unconventional use of the symbols does not necessarily mean that students did not understand their work throughout the lesson.

Reflect

When can you imagine needing to find a fraction of a whole number? Write you own fraction multiplication problem and solve it.

Number Visuals Sheet

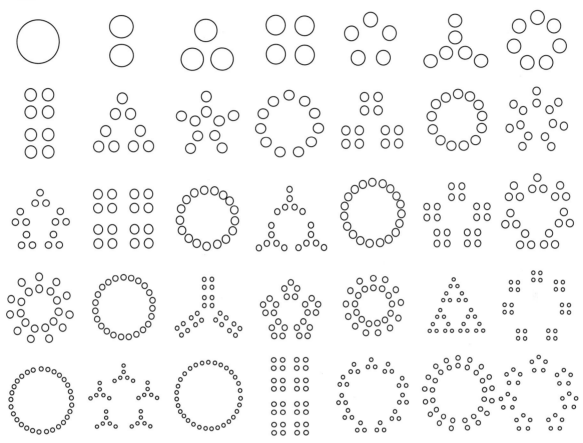

Number Visual Cards

Number Visual Cards

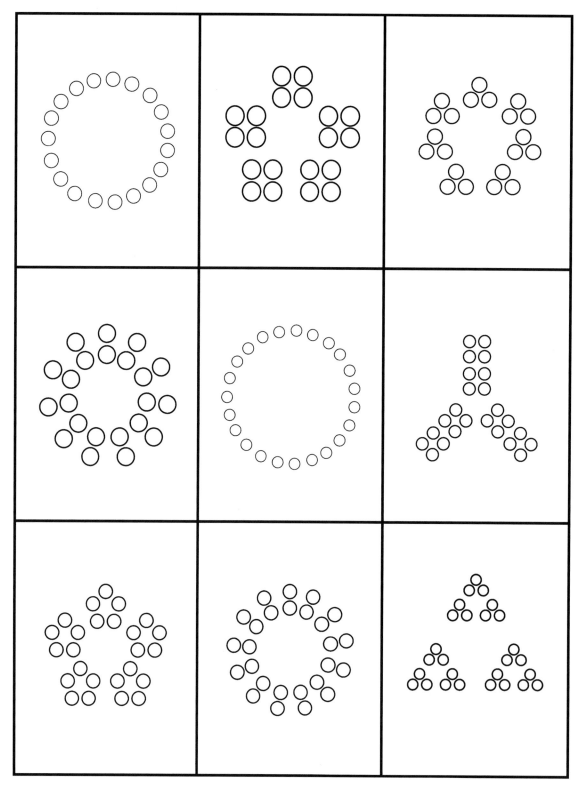

Mindset Mathematics, Grade 5, copyright © 2018 by Jo Boaler, Jen Munson, Cathy Williams.
Reproduced by permission of John Wiley & Sons, Inc.

Number Visual Cards

BIG IDEA 7

What Does It Mean to Divide Fractions?

"What does it mean to divide fractions?" is the name of this big idea, and it is also a very good question! Many people—adults as well as children—are confused by the question, which is not surprising, as dividing by fractions is something we rarely do in our lives. When posed a problem such as 1 divided by $\frac{1}{3}$, many people will interpret the problem as $1 \times \frac{1}{3}$. Liping Ma, in her book *Knowing and Teaching Elementary Mathematics,* found this to be true even among elementary teachers. When US elementary teachers were given questions requiring them to divide by a fraction, many of them multiplied by the fraction. Ma compared US teachers with teachers from China and found that the teachers from China were completely different. These teachers were able to divide by fractions and didn't multiply them, as the education system of China teaches deep, conceptual understanding of what it calls fundamental mathematics. The teachers in China do not attempt to know, nor are they pressured to know, as US teachers are, higher-level mathematics. But they have a rich, connected understanding of elementary mathematics. It is this conceptual understanding that we hope to encourage in these books, for teachers and students.

One way to divide by fractions is to "flip and multiply," but new research has shown that the concepts students need in order to use this algorithm with understanding extend beyond those they will have learned by fifth grade (Cordero, 2017). If students use the algorithm without understanding, they are vulnerable to thinking of math as a subject of nonsensical rules that they are meant to remember and use

199

but not understand, which is dangerous thinking. We want students to be engaged in sense making all the time and to see mathematics as a sense-making subject. In this big idea, we have worked to create situations and puzzles that will give students an understanding of what is happening when they divide by a fraction. Students will visualize the process and see the result. Hard thinking may be required—which is good, as that will enable synapses and neurons to spark and fire in students' brains!

In our Visualize activity, students will be thinking about making cards. This sets up a real situation that involves the division of fractions to be modeled for students. It also enables students to make choices as they make different cards, which can be all sorts of shapes. It will be good for students to realize that when they divide by $\frac{1}{3}$, the number gets bigger. Up until this time, they may have only encountered division making numbers smaller, so it is helpful to point out that when we divide by a number like $\frac{1}{3}$, our answer is a higher number than we started with, and to ask them to think about that: Why does that happen? That thinking is at the heart of all three of the activities in this big idea.

In our Play activity, students will be asked to work with Cuisenaire rods, which are a wonderful manipulative for mathematics learning at any age. Holding and moving the rods as students think about fraction division will use different areas of the brain and deepen understanding. We have asked students to build with the rods and record their discoveries in tables, which will also encourage brain connections to develop.

In our Investigate activity, students will be asked to look for patterns that they can see when they divide numbers. As they think in general terms about when they get odd numbers as results, they will be gaining a lot of good experience with the division of fractions and may be able to move beyond specific answers to see patterns. This will really help them stand back and understand the process of dividing by fractions. We also invite students to make conjectures, thinking ahead to what will happen with different numbers. This is an opportunity for students to generalize and to think like mathematicians.

Jo Boaler

Creating Cards

Snapshot

We begin to explore fraction division by making cards and cutting paper so that students can develop intuition about what division with fractions means.

Connection to CCSS
5.NF.7b,c

Agenda

Activity	Time	Description/Prompt	Materials
Launch	5 min	Show students a sheet of fancy paper and tell them you have 6 sheets for making cards. How many cards can you make if it takes $\frac{1}{3}$ of a sheet to make a card?	One sheet of fancy paper
Explore	15 min	Partners use paper and drawing to reason about dividing 6 sheets into cards of $\frac{1}{3}$ of a piece of paper each.	• Creating Cards Recording Sheet, one per partnership • Blank paper • Scissors
Discuss	15 min	Discuss the strategies and solutions students came up with. Reason about what number sentence(s) could be used to label what is happening. Establish this work as division with fractions and introduce the next exploration.	Chart and markers
Explore	20–30 min	Partners change the size of the cards, making them smaller or larger by choosing a different fraction of paper to use for a single card. They then investigate how this new card size changes the number of cards that can be made with 6 sheets of paper.	• Creating Larger or Smaller Cards Recording Sheet, one or more per partnership • Blank paper • Scissors

(Continued)

Activity	Time	Description/Prompt	Materials
Discuss	15 min	Record in a shared class table the different fractions students investigated and their results. Use the table to discuss patterns that emerge about changes in the number of cards made. Students also consider how to reason about remainders.	Chart and markers
Extend	15+ min	Students brainstorm other situations in which they might divide a whole number by a fraction.	

To the Teacher

This activity centers on making cards and using paper as a model for dividing a whole number by a unit fraction. Students in your community might have different traditions for making cards, or you may be teaching this lesson at a time of year when cards are often exchanged, such as Valentine's Day. Perhaps there is an event in your school for which students might make invitations, or a community-based holiday, or a tradition of recognizing students on their birthdays or as Student of the Week. We also know that the observance of holidays varies across communities, so we have refrained from naming a reason for making cards in this activity. We encourage you to tailor the context for card making in this activity so that it makes sense for your students.

A critical component to this lesson is developing intuition about fraction division, which for so many people defies reason. Students are likely to have learned that dividing gives a smaller answer or is about making things smaller, which does not always work with fractions. Algorithms for whole-number division also cannot be generalized to fraction division. Students often end up learning tricks that they do not understand, making errors they will not notice. In this lesson, we strive to build an intuitive sense of what is happening when we ask how many fractions fit inside a whole number. Students need to be able to cut real paper or draw rectangles to represent paper to help them reason about and justify their solutions. This context can serve as an anchor when they think about problems in the future so that they can imagine what is happening physically with the numbers and use rectangles to help them model. We encourage you to slow way down on these tasks and push students to reason about what is happening and how they know it makes sense.

Activity

Launch

Launch the lesson by showing students a piece of fancy paper. It could be a piece of construction paper that you have in class or something more elaborate. Tell them you are getting ready to make cards to give to friends and family. You have 6 sheets of this fancy paper that you can use, and you know you can make a card with $\frac{1}{3}$ of a piece of paper. Ask, How many cards can I make with my paper? How do you know? What shape could the cards be?

Explore

Students work in partners to figure out how many cards can be made with 6 sheets of paper if it takes $\frac{1}{3}$ of a sheet to make a single card. Provide them with paper (of any sort) to use to model the task and explore the shapes the cards might take. Ask students to record evidence of their solution on the Creating Cards Recording Sheet.

Once students have found one solution, encourage them to think about the different-shaped cards they might make. Ask, Does the shape of the cards change how many cards you can make?

Discuss

Once students have had a chance to explore this first problem, bring them together to discuss the following questions. Be sure to record students' thinking on a chart for future reference, along with examples of the models they use as evidence.

- How many cards can we make?
- How do you know? How did you know your answer made sense?
- How did you approach solving this problem?
- What number sentences can we use to label what we've done?
- What shape could the cards be? How do we know that each card is $\frac{1}{3}$?
- Does changing the shape of the card change the number of cards that you can make?

When you discuss how to label students' thinking with number sentences, be sure to open up debate, if it exists, about what operation you are engaging in and how it is recorded. Encourage the class to reason about the operation and whether students' suggested number sentences match what is happening. It is important that during this lesson, students come to see the work they do in this task as dividing a whole number by a fraction. Students may ask questions about how it is possible that 6 divided by $\frac{1}{3}$ could be a number as large as 18. We encourage you to explore this as a class and reason about why it makes sense. This challenges much of what students understand about division.

Explore

Pose the question to students, What if we changed the fraction of a piece of paper we used to make one card? Students work in partners to explore what happens when they make their cards larger or smaller. Encourage students to try some different fractions.

- What fraction of a piece of paper would you use to make a card?
- If you still have 6 sheets of fancy paper, now how many cards can you make?
- What shape could the cards be?

For each fraction students try, ask students to record their thinking on the Creating Larger and Smaller Cards Recording Sheets. Ask students to label their results with number sentences.

Discuss

Once students have had a chance to try several different fractions and to reason about their results, gather students together with their evidence to discuss the following questions. Make a chart or table for recording students' solutions for the different fractions they tried, similar to the one shown in Figure 7.1, which the group can use to search for overarching patterns.

- What fraction did you choose? How many cards could you make?
- What strategies did you use to solve this problem?
- How did the number of cards you could make change when you changed the fraction of paper needed to make a card? Why did it change?
- What is left over? Did anyone have leftover paper? How much? How did you know?

Students may notice the relationship between the size of the fraction and the number of cards they can make. Students may also begin to reason about the

Fraction Needed to Make One Card	Number of Cards Made	Leftover Paper	Number Sentence

Figure 7.1 Making Cards Recording Chart

relationship between the number of sheets of paper, the fraction, and the number of cards. Be cautious if students only choose to explore unit fractions, because students might overgeneralize the relationship, thinking that they can simply multiply the whole number by the denominator (for instance, $6 \div \frac{1}{3} = 18$ because $6 \times 3 = 18$). Highlight any examples of nonunit fractions to help students reason about those kinds of situations. If students have not chosen to explore these kinds of fractions, you might deliberately prompt them to think about what happens when it takes $\frac{2}{3}$ or $\frac{3}{4}$ or $\frac{3}{5}$ of a piece of paper to make a card, and send students back to explore these situations before returning to the discussion.

Extend

Ask students to generate other situations in which they might divide a whole number by a fraction. Encourage students to brainstorm as many possibilities as they can. Students might create general situations or write specific problems. In either case, the goal is for students to move beyond the specific case of making cards to considering how this kind of fraction division occurs throughout their world. Be sure to have students share their examples with the class to support all students in making connections.

Look-Fors

- **How are students labeling their work with number sentences?** Sometimes students' visual models are accurate and demonstrate their reasoning, but when they return to label their work with a number sentence, they might do so unconventionally, labeling their work as $\frac{1}{3} \div 6 = 18$ or even $6 \times 3 = 18$. Honor the sense that students have made in their work before turning toward the conventions. If, as in $\frac{1}{3} \div 6 = 18$, students have simply inverted the number sentence, ask them what it means when we say that one number is being "divided by" another, and then ask whether this matches what they have written. Students will often catch the misconception when they are asked to think aloud. In the case of $6 \times 3 = 18$, this is very likely what students were thinking and it makes sense, but it is not precisely what is happening in this situation. Point out that 3 isn't in the situation and ask where it came from. You might ask what happened to $\frac{1}{3}$ and whether there is a way to write a number sentence that uses $\frac{1}{3}$. The similarity between 6×3 and $6 \div \frac{1}{3}$ is an important one to discuss as a class and then to complicate later by looking at nonunit fractions.

- **Are students attempting to use an algorithm?** Some students may have had exposure to fraction algorithms without the opportunity to make sense of them, and these students might try to solve this problem algorithmically. A common error in this case is $6 \div \frac{1}{3} = \frac{1}{18}$. Challenge students to draw a picture to show what is happening in the situation and why their solution makes sense. You might ask, Does it make sense that I can make $\frac{1}{18}$ of a card with my 6 sheets of paper? Push students to reason about the numbers using the context of the situation, and then be sure to raise this as something for the class to think about in the discussion.

- **Are students overgeneralizing the division pattern and ignoring the numerator?** The potential challenge of exploring only unit fractions is that students will come to see $6 \div \frac{1}{3}$ as equal to 6×3 and learn to simply multiply the denominator by the whole number. The most straightforward way to avoid overgeneralizing this important pattern (for instance, students thinking that $6 \div \frac{3}{4} = 6 \times 4$) is simply to make sure that students have the chance to grapple with nonunit fractions and see what happens. If students do make this error, support them in using reasoning and models to determine whether it makes sense. That is, if each card gets bigger and is now $\frac{3}{4}$ of a piece of paper, does it make sense that we would be able to make more cards? What would it look like to cut the paper into cards?

Reflect

Why is it that division with fractions can lead to a larger answer than you started with?

Creating Cards Recording Sheet

Sketch how you divide your paper and then answer these questions:

- What fraction of the paper is needed to make one card?

- How many cards can you make with 6 sheets of paper?

- Did you use all of your paper? Was there any left over? How much was left over?

⬤ Creating Larger or Smaller Cards Recording Sheet

Sketch how you divide your paper and then answer these questions:

- What fraction of the paper is needed to make one card?

- How many cards can you make with 6 sheets of paper?

- Did you use all of your paper? Was there any left over? How much was left over?

Mindset Mathematics, Grade 5, copyright © 2018 by Jo Boaler, Jen Munson, Cathy Williams. Reproduced by permission of John Wiley & Sons, Inc.

Cuisenaire Trains

Snapshot

Students use Cuisenaire rods to explore the patterns that emerge when dividing a fraction into equal-size pieces.

Connection to CCSS
5.NF.7a,c

Agenda

Activity	Time	Description/Prompt	Materials
Launch	10 min	Show students an image of a Cuisenaire train in which the largest rod represents $\frac{1}{2}$, and ask students to discuss the values of the other rods shown. Record student thinking in a class table. Introduce the exploration.	• Cuisenaire rods • Cuisenaire Train image • Chart set up as a table, or a copy of the Playing with Cuisenaire Trains Recording Sheet • Markers
Play	30 min	Partners choose a starting rod and assign it a unit fraction value: $\frac{1}{2}$, $\frac{1}{3}$, $\frac{1}{4}$, $\frac{1}{5}$, $\frac{1}{6}$, or $\frac{1}{8}$. Then they build Cuisenaire trains and determine the values of the other, smaller rods in their trains. As they play with different values and rods, they record their findings in a table and look for patterns.	• Cuisenaire rod sets, one per partnership • Playing with Cuisenaire Trains Recording Sheet, one per student
Discuss	15+ min	Discuss the different values students found, recording them in the class chart, and the strategies students developed. Discuss the patterns students notice in their charts and the class chart. Do these patterns always work?	• Class chart and markers • Cuisenaire rods

(Continued)

Activity	Time	Description/Prompt	Materials
Extend	20+ min	Students may want to extend the puzzle to see whether the patterns noticed work for all unit fractions, even less-friendly fractions such as $\frac{1}{7}$.	• Cuisenaire rod sets, one per partnership • Playing with Cuisenaire Trains Recording Sheet, one per student

To the Teacher

A small note on language in this lesson: When taking the larger Cuisenaire rod, such as the purple one we designated as $\frac{1}{2}$ in the launch, and lining up smaller, same-size rods to create the same length, we have used the term *partition* to describe this action. It is tempting to say that we are *dividing* the larger rod *into* smaller parts, because this is how we might say it in conversation. However, in mathematics, "dividing into" has the opposite meaning; think about what we mean when we say, "I divided 4 into 16." The order makes a difference, and for the first time, students are working with numbers that can be divided in either order, each getting a different answer. Students can divide 2 by $\frac{1}{4}$ and find 8, or divide $\frac{1}{4}$ by 2 and find $\frac{1}{8}$. When students were working only with whole numbers, only one order made sense, and we all knew what they meant, even when we slipped with the language. When working with division of fractions, we encourage you to be careful about the language of division and help students pay attention to this language, too. This precision will help students build and maintain models of what is happening and describe it deliberately.

Activity

Launch

Launch this activity by reminding students of the work they did in the Visualize activity, using whole sheets of paper and figuring out how many fraction pieces would fit inside. Tell students that today we are going to explore what happens when we start with fractional pieces—instead of whole pieces—and look at what is inside them. Hold up a purple Cuisenaire rod and tell students that you decided this rod was $\frac{1}{2}$, and then you were wondering what would fit inside it. Show students the Cuisenaire Train image in Figure 7.2, of one purple, two red, and four white Cuisenaire rods stacked on top of each other, or you might use a document camera to show actual rods arranged in this way.

Tell students that you started with a purple rod and you partitioned it into equal parts in two different ways. If the purple is worth $\frac{1}{2}$, what is the value of the red rod? What is the value of the white rod? Give students time to turn and talk to a partner, then lead a brief discussion about the values. Be sure to support students in reasoning about the values. Some students may want to show what they are imagining in their minds by drawing, annotating the image, or adding new blocks.

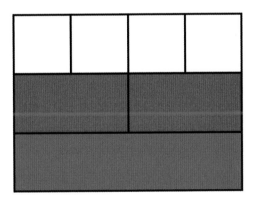

Figure 7.2 Cuisenaire Train

Record students' thinking in a table that mirrors the Playing with Cuisenaire Trains Recording Sheet or on a copy of the recording sheet itself, if you can show it on a document camera.

If I start with a ___ and I assume it's worth ___ . . .	Then I can partition it equally into . . .	So, each of these blocks is worth . . .
Purple = $\frac{1}{2}$	2 reds	Red = $\frac{1}{4}$
Purple = $\frac{1}{2}$	4 whites	White = $\frac{1}{8}$

What patterns can we find when we partition fractions? Tell students that today they will get to build Cuisenaire trains like the one in the image and decide what the value of the starting rod is. Students record their findings on the Playing with Cuisenaire Trains Recording Sheet to help them hunt for patterns.

Play

Provide partners with a set of Cuisenaire rods and a copy of the Playing with Cuisenaire Trains Recording Sheet for each student. Students start by choosing a rod and a unit fraction that it could represent: $\frac{1}{2}, \frac{1}{3}, \frac{1}{4}, \frac{1}{5}, \frac{1}{6}$, or $\frac{1}{8}$. They record this starting point in the left column of their table. Then students explore the following questions:

- If you want to partition this rod into equal parts using other Cuisenaire rods, how many different ways could you do it?
- How many parts could it be partitioned into?
- What is the value of each of these smaller rods? How do you know?

For each way they find to partition the rod they selected into smaller rods, students record their findings on the recording sheet. You may want students to sketch the trains they make on the back of the recording sheet as a way to remember what they were thinking or as a tool for figuring out the value of each rod piece.

As students begin to accumulate findings in their charts, encourage them to look for patterns. Ask, What do you notice? What patterns do you see? How could you use the Cuisenaire rods to see whether those patterns are always true?

Discuss

Once students have had a chance to build several Cuisenaire trains, puzzle out the fraction values of the pieces, and hunt for patterns, gather them together to discuss the following questions:

- What interesting solutions did you find? (Record these on your shared chart. You may also want students to model the trains they are talking about with Cuisenaire rods so that everyone can see what they found.)
- How did you figure out what each rod was worth? What strategies did you develop?
- What patterns did you notice when partitioning the rods? What patterns did you notice in your (or our) table?
- Which rods had the most solutions? Which rods had the fewest? Why do you think that is?
- Which fractions were the easiest to start with? Which were hardest? Why?

As you discuss these questions, be sure to dwell on observations of patterns that go across the rows of the Playing with Cuisenaire Trains Recording Sheet (that is, the relationship between the starting fraction, the number of smaller rods, and their value) and relationships students notice between rows (for instance, when you double the number of smaller rods, you halve their value).

Extend

Some students may wonder, Does this work for all unit fractions? In this lesson, we focused on unit fractions that are somewhat friendlier. Students may notice that we did not include $\frac{1}{7}$, for instance. Does this mean that these patterns don't work with $\frac{1}{7}$? Or $\frac{1}{9}$? Or what about $\frac{1}{20}$? If students begin to probe these what-if questions, consider following their inquiry and extending this puzzle to include any unit fraction students would like to explore. You will likely need more copies of the recording sheet.

Look-Fors

- **How are students using number sentences to label?** Some students may use number sentences to label the work they are doing, record their thinking, or describe a pattern they notice. Students may use a variety of number sentences, including multiplication (for instance, $\frac{1}{4} \times 2 = \frac{1}{2}$), addition ($\frac{1}{4} + \frac{1}{4} = \frac{1}{2}$), or division. If students use division, they may invert the number sentence as they try to figure out how to use symbols to represent what they have done. Students might, for instance, label our launch problem as $2 \div \frac{1}{2} = \frac{1}{4}$, instead of $\frac{1}{2} \div 2 = \frac{1}{4}$. In either case, use it as a moment to connect the meaning of the symbols back to the model of the Cuisenaire rods. What is happening with the rods? What does the number sentence say? You may find using whole numbers as an analogy helps student think through the connection and the meaning of their division number sentence. This is an important tool that you can make explicit to students: using a simpler case to help you think about a more complex case. For instance, if the rod were worth 12 and we fit 2 equal rods inside it, how much would each rod be worth? And how would we write the division number sentence? How can that help us think about what is happening with the fractions?

- **How are students finding the value of the smaller rods?** Some students may be able to assign a starting value to a rod and build a train, but then struggle to determine the value of the smaller rods. Ask students how they might be able to use the rods to see the value more clearly. Many students benefit from adding onto the train to see a whole, which helps them prove the value of each rod. You might return to the example train from the launch and ask students how they might prove that the red is worth $\frac{1}{4}$ to someone who is not convinced. Students will often elaborate by drawing, adding rods on, or using some additional reasoning. You can then ask them how these same strategies might help them with the current train. If many students are struggling, you might pull the class together to hear a few strategies from students who had some ideas, before sending students back to work.

Reflect

What is happening when we take a fraction and divide it by a whole number? Draw a picture or use an example to help you describe what is happening.

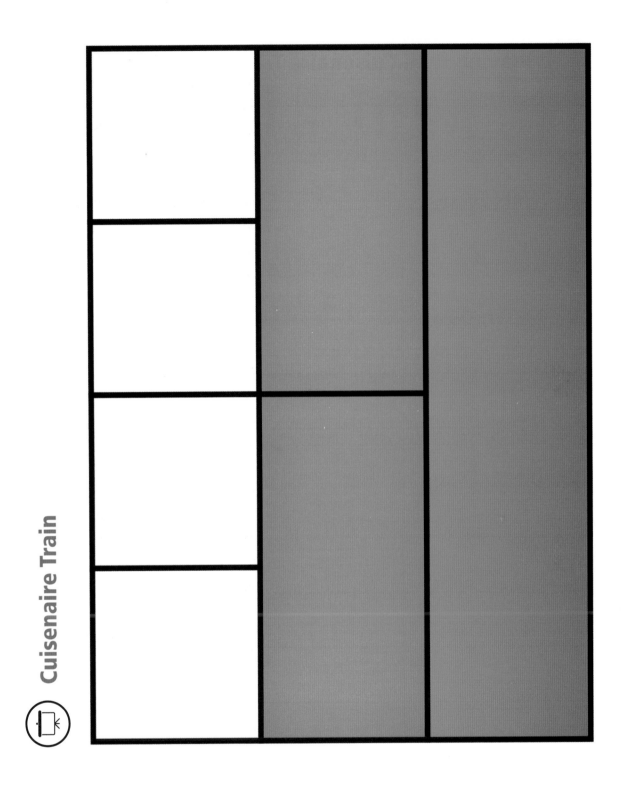

Cuisenaire Train

If I start with a ___ and I assume it's worth ___ . . .	Then I can partition it equally into . . .	So, each of these blocks is worth . . .
Purple = $\frac{1}{2}$	2 reds	Red = $\frac{1}{4}$

Fraction Division Conundrum

Snapshot

Students divide whole numbers by unit fractions to investigate when the quotients are even and when they are odd. They develop visual proofs for dividing these numbers and conjectures for the patterns they notice.

Connection to CCSS
5.NF.7b
5.OA.3

Agenda

Activity	Time	Description/Prompt	Materials
Launch	5 min	Show students a visual proof for $3 \div \frac{1}{4} = 12$. Note that starting with an odd number, we get an even quotient.	Chart and markers
Explore	20+ mins	Partners investigate the following questions: What even numbers can you get by dividing 3 by a unit fraction? What patterns do you notice in your solutions?	
Discuss	15 min	Discuss what other even numbers students found when dividing 3 by a unit fraction. Organize students' findings on a chart or on paper and look for patterns.	Chart or blank paper, and markers
Explore	30+ min	Partners divide a whole number from 1 to 9 by a unit fraction to investigate when it results in an even or an odd number. Students develop conjectures, make predictions about dividing larger numbers, and test them. Partners create a poster to show their conjecture and the evidence they have gathered to support or contradict it.	Chart and markers for each partnership
Discuss	20 min	Post students' charts and have them do a gallery walk, looking for shared observations and interesting ideas to pursue. Discuss the patterns students noticed when dividing whole numbers by unit fractions and what they are wondering now.	Student charts

To the Teacher

In this investigation, we connect fraction division, multiplication, and properties of numbers with patterning, proof, and the development of conjectures. By examining fraction division from the curious lens that asks, "What happens if...?", students generate ideas, questions, and evidence that enable them to see the underlying structure of dividing whole numbers by unit fractions, which we began to uncover in the Visualize activity. Students may build on the ideas and visual models they developed in that earlier activity to create visual proofs that show why a division problem, such as $3 \div \frac{1}{4}$, is equivalent to 3×4. Then students will draw on and ask questions about ideas of even and odd that they likely discussed in much earlier grades, but not yet in the context of operations with fractions.

This investigation can stretch across two days as students generate and solve their own problems, looking for patterns. Encourage students to document their findings in ways that are clear, organized, and convincing. If students develop their own lines of inquiry during the lesson, we encourage you to let students pursue them. Perhaps they will build on ideas of properties of numbers and ask, Can you ever get a prime quotient when dividing a whole number by a unit fraction? Or, Does this work for nonunit fractions? Genuine wonder should be encouraged and celebrated.

Activity

Launch

Launch the lesson by showing students that if we divide 3 by $\frac{1}{4}$, we get 12. Draw a visual proof that there are 12 fourths inside of 3, like the one shown in Figure 7.3. You might remind students of the work they did in the Visualize activity modeling making cards and the different ways they showed their thinking.

Notice aloud that starting with an odd number, 3, we can get an even quotient, 12. Ask: Will that always happen? What other even numbers could you get by dividing 3 by a unit fraction?

Explore

Students work with a partner to investigate these questions:

- What even numbers can you get by dividing 3 by a unit fraction?
- What patterns do you notice in your solutions?

Partners write and solve their own problems to figure out what is possible. Students record their findings using visual proofs so that they can look for patterns and share with others.

Discuss

Gather students together to discuss what even numbers they were able to generate by dividing 3 by a unit fraction. Record students' findings, including the number sentences and visual proofs. You may want to record these results on a chart, or you could record them on individual pieces of paper so that they can be sorted, ordered, or grouped. Looking at students' findings, ask, What patterns do you notice?

Pose the next part of the investigation by asking students to investigate how we get even or odd results from dividing whole numbers by unit fractions.

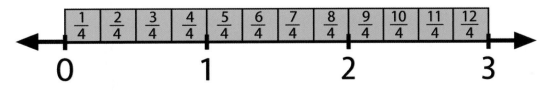

Figure 7.3 Visual Proof That 3 Divided by $\frac{1}{4}$ Equals 12

Explore

Students work with their partners to investigate what numbers they can generate by dividing a whole number from 1 to 9 by a unit fraction. Encourage students to develop ways of organizing and recording their results so that they can look for patterns. Some students may want to use a table to organize their findings. Others might prefer recording each finding on a sticky note or index card so that they can group or arrange them in different ways to see patterns. Be sure to support students in thinking about what ways will work best for them. Ask students to investigate the following questions:

- When are the results odd?
- When are the results even?
- How can you organize your findings to help you see patterns? What patterns do you notice?

Ask student to use their findings to make a conjecture about dividing larger numbers (such as numbers between 10 and 19 or between 20 and 29) by unit fractions. Conjectures are statements that might answer the following questions:

- When would you predict an odd quotient?
- When would you predict an even quotient?
- Do you think the patterns you've noticed will be the same no matter how large the whole number or how small the unit fraction? Why or why not?

Ask students to make a poster showing their conjecture and the evidence they have gathered to support their thinking, including visual representations.

Discuss

Gather students and their evidence together. Have partners post their charts around the room and then have students do a gallery walk to look for patterns many of them have noticed and patterns that they want to explore more.

Discuss the following questions as a class:

- What patterns did you discover dividing whole numbers by unit fractions? What evidence do you have for these patterns? Why do you think these patterns exist?

- Why are the quotients sometimes even and sometimes odd? How can we predict what the result will be?
- What patterns did you see on your classmates' charts that you think are worth discussing, either because they are interesting or because you're not sure whether you agree? (Take some time to discuss these patterns.)
- What are you wondering now?

If students come up with different-looking charts and different visual representations, celebrate this. Tell students that this is part of the beauty of mathematics: that we can see and represent it in different ways.

Look-Fors

- **Are students creating meaningful models of fraction division?** Building on the Visualize activity, students have generated some visual models of fraction division, namely by subdividing rectangular regions. You may see some students using this as a visual proof. Others may develop other methods for showing visually the process of division. In either case, notice their models carefully and ask whether and how they match the division they are intended to represent. Sometimes students subdivide regions inaccurately, especially when they do so repetitively, and errors will make conjectures more difficult to generate.

- **Are students connecting fraction division to whole-number multiplication?** The notion that $3 \div \frac{1}{4}$ can also be thought of 3×4 is an important connection for students to make, grounded in the visual representations that show why this makes sense. As you look at how students are solving, notice the language and equivalencies they are using that build the bridge between $3 \div \frac{1}{4}$ and 3×4. In particular, students may see that there are 4 fourths in each whole, so 3×4 is 12, which connects to the idea that $\frac{12}{4} = 3$, so $\frac{12}{4} \div \frac{1}{4}$ is also 12. When students begin to notice these features, ask questions about why they make sense and what they mean for the idea of dividing with fractions.

- **How are students reasoning about the even and odd results?** Part of finding the pattern in even and odd results is attending to the even and odd properties of the numbers being divided. Fractions themselves, as nonwhole numbers, are not even or odd, but their numerators and denominators can be called even or odd. Students will need to think about these properties and ask why such patterns emerge, which may push on knowledge developed in earlier grades about even and odd. Some students may have been asked to memorize even and odd only as an alternating pattern in the counting sequence, but understanding the patterns here will prompt students to think more deeply about what makes a number even or odd. You may want to ask students: What does it mean that a number is even or odd? How could you show even or odd with a picture or objects? How does that connect with the operation of division (or multiplication)?

- **How are students collecting and organizing their findings?** To see patterns, students will need to develop ways that make sense to them to organize what they find. They may develop systems for investigation—for example, to pursue a single whole number and try unit fractions in decreasing size from $\frac{1}{2}$ to $\frac{1}{3}$ to $\frac{1}{4}$, and so forth. They may instead fix on a unit fraction, such as $\frac{1}{2}$, and explore a variety of whole numbers into which it can be divided, from 1 to 2 to 3, and so forth. Some students may decide to compare cases they think will be meaningful, say by exploring even whole numbers and odd whole numbers in two groups. However, as they proceed, they will need to record these findings in ways that enable them to see or hunt for patterns. Some students may prefer to put their results on individual papers or sticky notes so that they can rearrange and organize them flexibly. Others may prefer a table or other tool for structuring their findings. Support students in thinking about what they want to do as they begin to accumulate findings.

Reflect

What patterns would you predict if you divided a unit fraction by a whole number? Why?

References

Cordero, M. (2017). *It's (not) ours to reason why: A comparative analysis of algorithms for the division of fractions* (Unpublished honors thesis). Stanford University, Stanford, CA.

Ma, L. (2010). *Knowing and teaching elementary mathematics: Teachers' understanding of fundamental mathematics in China and the United States* (2nd ed.). New York, NY: Routledge.

Thinking in Powers of 10

Students are fascinated by really big and really small numbers, and as we work to introduce students to the mathematical ways of recording them, we should aim to keep their fascination and wonder alive. As I was writing this introduction, I saw a photograph that a first-grade teacher had posted on Instagram, from a project he calls "A First Grader's Guide to the Galaxy." I love the posters of stars that the young children made, and it reminded me how much children are enthralled by the galaxy and that so many stars can be seen. This is a lovely example of a situation with a really big number, which could be used to introduce this big idea.

Our three activities for this big idea all aim to capture students' imagination about really big and small numbers, focusing their learning in situations that they will wonder about and be curious about, and even want to share with their family and friends.

In the Visualize activity, we introduce students to the ideas of very big and small numbers, introducing a unit of measurement—someone's height—and then asking students to find examples that are 10, 100, and 1,000 times bigger and smaller. Students can use different ways to record their ideas—words, diagrams, photographs, and actual models—creating a display for others to see. They may even want to create a tour for others to walk around the school to see different objects.

In the Play activity, students get further opportunities to extend this thinking, and we suggest that they are given the chance to make a movie to show what happens when something becomes much bigger or smaller. They can do this by zooming in or out, with an iPad or other camera. This will be a really nice activity for students

Source: Matt Sheelen

and will also provide the perfect opportunity for thinking about what happens when objects become bigger or smaller.

In the Investigate activity, we introduce the naming of "powers of 10" and ask students to create a Museum of the Very Large and Small for visitors. Encourage students to find examples that will be interesting and perhaps surprising for visitors. As students work to make an interesting exhibit, help them see the value and need for powers of 10 as a way of recording. This should be a deeply engaging activity for students and one that gives them an opportunity to be proud of the new mathematical ways of recording that they have learned.

Jo Boaler

The Unit You

Snapshot

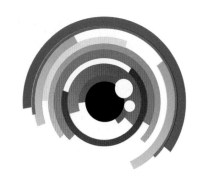

Students explore the relationship between powers of 10 from $\frac{1}{1,000}$ to 1,000 by creating visual references, beginning with a student's height as the unit. Groups present their findings using objects, drawings, and photos, and by marking physical spaces in the classroom and school.

> **Connection to CCSS**
> 5.NBT.1
> 5.NBT.2

Agenda

Activity	Time	Description/Prompt	Materials
Launch	10 min	Tell students that the numbers $\frac{1}{1,000}$, $\frac{1}{100}$, $\frac{1}{10}$, 1, 10, 100, and 1,000, which they have been working to make friendly since first grade, are all connected. This activity will explore their relationship by using a student's height as the unit.	• Chart or board with the numbers $\frac{1}{1,000}$, $\frac{1}{100}$, $\frac{1}{10}$, 1, 10, 100, and 1,000 listed • Materials and resources for the activity to show
Explore	45+ min	Students work in small groups to select one member's height to be the unit. Then students work to identify objects or distances that represent $\frac{1}{1,000}$, $\frac{1}{100}$, $\frac{1}{10}$, 1, 10, 100, and 1,000 times that unit. Students design ways to share their findings using drawings, photos, words, and objects.	• A variety of materials for representing, marking, and recording measurements, such as masking tape, adding machine tape, chalk, beads, blocks, and cameras • Measurement tools, such as rules, yardsticks, and measuring tape • Tools for sharing findings, such as computers or charts and markers • Optional: Unit You Organizer, one per group

(Continued)

Activity	Time	Description/Prompt	Materials
Discuss	20+ min	Groups share their various findings, their processes, and their thinking about moving between values. Discuss the relationships between the values.	Class table or display for sharing groups' findings

To the Teacher

This activity centers on using students' own heights as a unit to explore powers of 10, particularly with $\frac{1}{1,000}$, $\frac{1}{100}$, $\frac{1}{10}$, 1, 10, 100, and 1,000. We don't often get the chance to see all of these values side by side, which can limit our understanding of their magnitude. In this activity, by using the same unit to visualize all of the numbers, students can better see the relationships and think about how they move from one to another by multiplying or dividing by 10. Give some thought to the resources you have available that students can use to represent such large and small numbers. You may want to have some very small objects on hand, such as dried beans or rice, beads, or blocks. Students will need tools for measuring and marking, such as rulers, yardsticks, measuring tape, adding machine tape, masking tape, or chalk. Students may want to mark a distance in the hallway or on a wall; masking tape can be a good tool for this. If students want to mark a distance outside, sidewalk chalk can also be useful. Adding machine tape can be used to create a "unit," making it easier to iterate that unit or fold it to find a fraction of it.

Groups will also need some options for how they might present their findings to the class. Students may want to take photographs and present these printed on a chart or in a slideshow. Alternatively, students could draw diagrams or use words to describe the largest distances on a chart. Students may want to show the objects themselves, particularly for the smaller values. For larger values, students may want to take a walking tour of spaces marked in the hallway or schoolyard. We have left these options open for you to decide, knowing that every school context is different.

We offer one final note on choosing students to be the unit in this project. Some students will be eager to be the focus of so much attention, delighted to have their group present the distance that is "10 Alexes long," for instance. But other students may be uncomfortable being center stage in this way, having their bodies measured by a classmate. We have deliberately designed this activity to account for these different responses to being the unit. We encourage you to support the groups in deciding who will serve as the unit, without the requirement that anyone has to be in that role. If no one in the group feels comfortable, you can simply offer them the height of a piece of furniture in your classroom or your own height to use. In all likelihood, many students will be excited to be the unit and imagine what 10 or 100 times their height looks like, or how tall they would be if shrunk to $\frac{1}{100}$ their current height.

Activity

Launch

Launch by recording the following numbers on a chart or board: $\frac{1}{1,000}$, $\frac{1}{100}$, $\frac{1}{10}$, 1, 10, 100, 1,000. Tell students that since first grade, they have been working to make these numbers friendly. We started with 10, then 100, then 1,000, growing our friendly numbers larger and larger. Then in fourth grade, students spent time thinking about zooming in on parts of numbers, and they worked to make the fractions $\frac{1}{10}$ and $\frac{1}{100}$ friendly. These numbers are all connected, and they have an important relationship.

Tell students that today we're going to explore that relationship by starting with you, the student, as our unit. Students will work in small groups, choosing one person who is willing to be the unit. This student's height will be the group's unit, or 1 whole. Using the materials you make available, the group figures out how to represent the numbers you've listed on the board ($\frac{1}{1,000}$, $\frac{1}{100}$, $\frac{1}{10}$, 1, 10, 100, and 1,000), with 1 being the height of one of the group members.

Groups need to create some way to share these findings—poster, photos, slideshow, diagram, and/or objects. Be sure to tell students what their parameters are for constructing representations given the resources you have available.

Explore

Students work in small groups of three to four and choose one willing member to be the unit, or 1 whole. Students should have access to measuring tools, chart paper, markers, everyday materials around the room, small objects, and spaces outside your classroom, such as the hallway or schoolyard. You might want to make available sidewalk chalk or masking tape for marking distances on the ground. If possible, make cameras available for documenting what students find. We encourage you to create a space where students can access the various materials you've made available for this activity.

Students will need to measure their unit in some way. Then the group works together to identify objects or distances that represent $\frac{1}{1,000}$, $\frac{1}{100}$, $\frac{1}{10}$, 10, 100, and 1,000 times the height of the person serving as the group's unit:

- What does $\frac{1}{1,000}$ of the unit look like?
- What does $\frac{1}{100}$ of the unit look like?
- What does $\frac{1}{10}$ of the unit look like?

- What does 10 times the unit look like?
- What does 100 times the unit look like?
- What does 1,000 times the unit look like?

Note that true precision is not possible, and students will need to decide what examples are close enough. For each value the group finds, students need to figure out how to represent that value so that they can share it with the class using photos, drawings, words, markings, or objects. Students might choose a variety of ways to show the different distances. For instance, for $\frac{1}{1,000}$, they may want to hold up an object; for 10, they may describe the distance in words (such as, "10 Alexes is the same as the distance from the door to the window in the corner"); and for 1,000, they may mark a distance in chalk on the schoolyard and take a picture. Multimedia sharing makes sense given the differences in magnitude and can be great fodder for discussion. Groups may benefit from the Unit You Organizer provided to help them remember and organize their findings. This organizer is optional and not meant to replace more visual forms of sharing; rather it can serve as a note-taking tool.

Discuss

Ask groups to share their findings. Instead of having each group share everything, have groups all share by number so that comparing is easier. Starting with the unit, first ask groups to share their representations of something smaller than the unit: $\frac{1}{10}$, $\frac{1}{100}$, and $\frac{1}{1,000}$. Then ask groups to share representations of the distances larger than their unit: 10, 100, and 1,000 times the length of the unit. You might want to create a class table of the objects or distances that the groups found to represent each distance, such as the one here:

$\frac{1}{1,000}$	$\frac{1}{100}$	$\frac{1}{10}$	1	10	100	1,000
Thickness of a grain of rice Thickness of a magazine	Unit cube from base 10 blocks Bead Thickness of a paperback novel	Half a floor tile Marker	Student names	Distance from classroom door to the bathroom Height of the school	Length of the football field including end zones Distance around the school building	Distance walking the fence around the school

Then discuss the following questions:

- How did you find your values? What strategies did you develop? How did you use tools to support your work?
- How are our representations for each value similar and different? Why?
- How did you think about moving from $\frac{1}{10}$ to $\frac{1}{100}$ to $\frac{1}{1,000}$ of the unit? What challenges did you face?
- How did you think about moving from 10 to 100 to 1,000 times the unit? What challenges did you face?
- What relationships did you notice? What surprised you?

Look-Fors

- **How are students thinking about multiplying or dividing the unit?** Some students may get tangled up trying to be very precise, and then get lost in calculations. Support students in developing ways not to think of their unit as, say, "55 inches," but as 1 whole. Encourage students to represent their whole as a physical unit, by taping rulers together or cutting a strip of adding machine tape or yarn. Having a physical unit will help students think about how they might iterate this unit to make more, or fold or cut the unit to make fractions of it.

- **Are students thinking about the values they find in relationship to one another?** How are students testing their ideas about small values? This is a place to encourage thinking about the relationships between the fractions. For instance, it is useful to think of $\frac{1}{10}$ as the height we can stack on top of each other 10 times to get back to the unit. Once you have $\frac{1}{10}$, you can think of $\frac{1}{10}$ of that to help you imagine what objects might be useful references for $\frac{1}{100}$. Students can test whether their $\frac{1}{100}$ makes sense by seeing whether 10 of those objects can be used to create $\frac{1}{10}$. Ask students probing questions about how they know their objects or distances work by asking students to use the relationships between the different objects they have selected.

- **How are students documenting their findings?** Encourage students to document both their process and their findings for sharing with other students. Support students in determining the most vivid way to present each value. The key question is, What will help other students really see what this value looks like? If students use words, encourage them to be as descriptive as possible so that others know, for instance, which door or wall they are refer-ring to when describing a distance as "from the door to the wall."

Reflect

What surprised you about the values you explored: $\frac{1}{1,000}$, $\frac{1}{100}$, $\frac{1}{10}$, 1, 10, 100, and 1,000? How are these numbers related?

The Unit You Organizer

Find objects that match the question for the unit value shown in each column and record them in the box. For each row, you will need to identify who is your unit value: Who is your 1?

What does $\frac{1}{1,000}$ look like?	What does $\frac{1}{100}$ look like?	What does $\frac{1}{10}$ look like?	Who is 1?	What does 10 look like?	What does 100 look like?	What does 1,000 look like?

Filling Small and Large

Snapshot

Students play with representing powers of 10 using small everyday objects and comparing the space taken up by 10, 100, 1,000, or more of those objects. They create ways of representing these quantities and of thinking about what $\frac{1}{10}$ or $\frac{1}{100}$ of a small object might look like. The class compares how these values, from $\frac{1}{100}$ to 1,000 and beyond, look when the units are different sizes.

Connection to CCSS
5.NBT.1
5.NBT.2

Agenda

Activity	Time	Description/Prompt	Materials
Launch	10 min	Remind students of the work they did to represent numbers from $\frac{1}{1,000}$ to 1,000 in the Visualize activity. Show students some small units to choose from and ask them to estimate the space taken up by 1,000 units.	Small units to show: blocks, tiles, paper clips, cereal, dried beans, toothpicks, and the like
Explore	30 min	Partners choose a unit and figure out how much space is taken up by 10, 100, 1,000, and a larger power of 10 of this unit. Students imagine what $\frac{1}{10}$ or $\frac{1}{100}$ of the unit would look like. Partners represent their findings to share with the class.	• Large quantities of small units, such as blocks, tiles, paper clips, cereal, dried beans, or toothpicks • Charts and markers for each partnership • Optional: containers of various sizes

(Continued)

Activity	Time	Description/Prompt	Materials
Discuss	15+ min	Partnerships pair up and share their findings. Create a class display of some examples of the space needed for quantities of different units. Discuss what students discovered, how their initial estimates compare with their findings, and how what they found was different from working with distance.	• Students' findings to share • Space to display samples of students' findings
Extend	30+ min	Small groups make a movie showing what happens when you make something—quantity, distance, or volume—bigger or smaller by 10.	• Technology for movie-making, such as tablets • Make available: objects (such as those in this activity), manipulatives, and measurement tools as needed

To the Teacher

In this activity, students are returning to the idea of making physical comparisons between powers of 10, from $\frac{1}{100}$ to 1,000 and beyond. In the Visualize activity, students used distance as a way of constructing references. Now we move into thinking about quantity and space (or volume). To set up, you will need units that are small, inexpensive, and countable, and that you can get in large quantities, such as blocks or other small manipulatives, toothpicks, dried pasta, rice, dried beans, marshmallows, cereal, gravel, paper clips, beads, or confetti. We encourage you to be creative with the objects and to offer some choice to students, if possible. Students will be using these as their units—a very different unit than the height of a student.

In the launch, we ask students to estimate how much space 1,000 of one of the available units will take up. We encourage you to use this as valuable formative assessment data. We have found that students often vastly overestimate what a group of 1,000 small objects looks like. Asking students to use their hands and arms to indicate how big the space would be will give you a quick visual assessment of how students are thinking about 1,000 and using the size of the unit to support their estimates. Estimating first also gives students something with which to compare their later findings, perhaps discovering that a group of 1,000 beads is not what they expected.

Source: Shutterstock.com/Oksana Shufrych

If you are exploring this big idea after learning about volume, you may want to draw on students' understanding of filling space using cubic units. The objects you are likely to use do not have an easy-to-measure volume individually, but as students move to 100 or more units, they can think about the cubic units filled by the objects. Alternately, you may have volume manipulatives that students can fill as a different way to measure the space. There is no need for students to calculate here, but finding additional references, such as a cube block, or a measuring cup, may make communicating about space clearer.

Activity

Launch

Launch this activity by reminding students of the work they did in the Visualize activity, which focused on using the length of a person's body as a unit and then finding lengths that were 10, 100, and 1,000 times and $\frac{1}{10}$, $\frac{1}{100}$, and $\frac{1}{1,000}$ as long. If you still have artifacts from this activity around the room, you might want to refer to them. Tell students that today we're going to play with what happens when we think not about length but about space, and explore what happens when we start with a much, much smaller unit.

Show students several units that they can choose from to explore. You might offer some manipulatives, such as blocks or tiles, and some everyday objects, such as paper clips or dried beans. Introduce the task.

Then ask students to turn and talk to a partner: choose a unit together and estimate how much space they think 1,000 of that unit will take up. Ask students to share some ideas and show with their hands the space they think 1,000 will fill. Tell students that it is now time to test their estimates.

Explore

Students work in partners, choosing a unit to explore. For their unit, partners explore the following questions:

- How much space or volume would 10 units fill?
- How much space or volume would 100 units fill?
- How much space or volume would 1,000 units fill?
- What about an even larger value? Choose a number like 10,000 or 100,000 to explore.

Students find a way of representing their findings for others to see. This might include drawings, numbers, and/or using containers as references. Students might find charts and markers useful, or have other ways they would like to represent what they have found.

Ask students, How could you represent the space that $\frac{1}{10}$ or $\frac{1}{100}$ of your unit would fill? Ask students to challenge themselves to find some way of showing what that space might look like and add this to their representation of larger numbers.

Students may want to play with a second unit and compare it with the first unit. For instance, they may want to see how 1,000 marshmallows compare to 1,000 grains of rice. If students try this, be sure to encourage them to document the differences they discover.

Discuss

Start the discussion by pairing up partnerships so that two pairs who explored different units can share their findings with one another. Ask students to compare their findings. Ask: How are the similar? How are they different? Why?

Then, as a whole class, discuss what students learned by comparing their models with others'. On a wall, board, or table, show some of the student-created examples for each number they explored: $\frac{1}{100}$, $\frac{1}{10}$, 10, 100, 1,000, and anything larger. Be sure to label each number. We encourage you to leave this display up for reference during the Investigate activity.

Discuss the following questions:

- What did you discover about these numbers? What surprised you? (Ask partners to share some of their most interesting findings with the class.)
- How did your estimations at the beginning of the lesson compare with your findings?
- Which units were the most interesting or challenging to work with? Why?
- All of our units were small, but they weren't the same size. How did the size of the unit affect what the values looked like?
- How was exploring space different from exploring with length? How was exploring with a large unit (a person) different from exploring with a small unit? How did it change your thinking about these values?

Extend

If students have access to tablets or other technology for making movies, you can invite them to make a short film showing what happens when we make something bigger or smaller by 10. You can leave this open to showing quantity, distance (as in the Visualize activity), or volume (as in this Play activity). Provide students with access to measurement tools, manipulatives, and the same small objects used in this lesson. Students may want to focus their movie on many jumps by 10 or just a few, such as from 1 to 10 to 100. Alternatively, students may want to show getting smaller by dividing by 10, moving from 1 to $\frac{1}{10}$ to $\frac{1}{100}$.

Look-Fors

- **Are students thinking about multiplying (or dividing) by 10 as they move from one representation to the next?** At the heart of this big idea is the multiplicative relationship between powers of 10. If students, say, count out 100 beans, they should be thinking about 1,000 beans as 10 groups the same size as the pile of 100. When trying to imagine $\frac{1}{10}$, students should be cutting that bean (mentally, or a drawing of it) into 10 equal parts. It makes sense for students to want to count out the quantities to see precisely how much space is taken up, but certainly beyond 1,000 they will have to imagine and estimate.

- **How are students expressing space?** There are lots of ways students might document how much space is taken up by different quantities of their units. Encourage students to think flexibly and critically about what might be the most useful or clearest representation. Students might describe in words, draw a picture, or find a container to serve as reference. Pictures might show a three-dimensional space (such as a box that is about $2 \times 2 \times 3$ inches) or delineate the region covered if the objects are packed in a single layer. Containers can be useful because it is often easier to imagine 10 containers as students try to move to the next power of 10.

- **Are students drawing comparisons between the different units explored?** Students will get to see several different units in this activity, and they used their own bodies as units in the Visualize activity. One goal is for students to see that the meaning of the numbers we work with depends on the unit. For instance, a string 1,000 Alexes long may encircle your school campus, but 1,000 paper clips can be held by one person. Seeing how differences in the unit size multiply into ever greater differences is important.

Reflect

What quantity or representation surprised you the most? Why?

Museum of the Very Large and Small
Snapshot

In this investigation, we name the numbers we have been learning about as "powers of 10" and investigate the meaning of very large and small powers of 10. Small groups choose a power of 10 and construct a museum exhibit to make their number's meaning clear, and the class stages a Museum of the Very Large and Small for visitors.

Connection to CCSS
5.NBT.1
5.NBT.2

Agenda

Activity	Time	Description/Prompt	Materials
Launch	15–20 min	Revisit earlier work with the numbers $\frac{1}{100}$, $\frac{1}{10}$, 1, 10, 100, and 1,000. Name these as "powers of 10," created by multiplying or dividing 1 repeatedly by 10. Watch the Eames film "Powers of Ten." Introduce the task of creating a museum, which makes even larger or smaller powers of 10 familiar.	Technology to show "Powers of Ten" video from website
Explore	60+ min	Small groups choose a very large or very small power of 10 to represent. Groups investigate the question, What does this number represent? Each group uses its findings to construct a museum exhibit about its number that makes the meaning of the number clear to others.	• Materials to construct exhibits: chart paper, cardboard, markers, scissors, tape, and butcher or construction paper • Manipulatives, such as base 10 blocks, cubes, tiles, or meter sticks • Optional: technology, such as cameras or tablets

(Continued)

Activity	Time	Description/Prompt	Materials
Present	30+ min	Arrange students' number exhibits for your museum opening. Invite visitors, such as other classes or families. All visitors use sticky notes to record responses to the exhibits and post them on a wall or board under "I'm surprised that . . ." and "I wonder . . ."	• Exhibits displayed for visitors • Sticky notes for all visitors • Space set up for sticky notes to be placed in two categories: "I'm surprised that . . ." and "I wonder . . ."
Discuss	20 min	Discuss in small groups and then as a whole class what students learned by constructing their exhibits and from visiting the exhibits of others. Examine the comments left by visitors, and discuss what visitors learned and wondered.	Sticky notes left by visitors
Extend	40+ min	If visitors left interesting, worthy questions, the class might choose to pursue investigating the most compelling ones.	

To the Teacher

This investigation requires an investment in materials and time. It will likely take at least two days to investigate numbers, construct exhibits, and stage the museum. We have listed a number of materials that you might want to make available to students to investigate the numbers, make models or displays, and construct exhibits. This list is intended to support you in thinking about the materials you have available in your school that you might access for this project. It is not meant to be exhaustive or required. We encourage you to think creatively about materials and space for constructing the museum. Displays could easily be made on existing bulletin boards or using recycled cardboard boxes. Students might opt to record on chart paper and have their displays on desk or table tops. You might consider soliciting recycled materials from students that could be used for displays, such as empty yogurt containers that students could fill with small objects.

We encourage you to make the museum as authentic as possible by inviting an audience, such as other classes in your school or students' families. If this activity takes place during a time in your school year when there are evening family events, you could open the museum for families then, too. Inviting visitors takes some advance planning, so you may want to coordinate with other teachers ahead of the lesson to ensure an audience.

Activity

Launch

Launch the lesson by reminding students of the work they did in the previous two activities building models by starting with a unit (a person or small object) and making it 10 times bigger or $\frac{1}{10}$ as big, again and again. Revisit the display you created as a class in the Play activity showing examples of the space taken up by $\frac{1}{100}$, $\frac{1}{10}$, 1, 10, 100, 1,000, or more units. Tell students that these numbers are called "powers of 10" and that they are created by starting with 1 and repeatedly multiplying or dividing by 10, a pattern students may have noticed as they built their models. Tell students that we use a special notation for this: exponents. Add a new label to your display for each number, showing it as a power of 10. For example, show $100 = 10 \times 10 = 10^2$ and $1,000 = 10 \times 10 \times 10 = 10^3$.

Tell students that this pattern of multiplying by 10 again and again can go on forever, well beyond the display you made as a class. Tell them they are going to watch a short video that explores how far you could go with this kind of exploration. Show the Charles and Ray Eames film "Powers of Ten," a nine-minute documentary that can be found online at www.eamesoffice.com/the-work/powers-of-ten/.

Tell students that for today's exploration, instead of choosing a unit to start with, they and their group will choose a number—either very large or very small—to investigate. Their goal is to find several ways to represent that number so that we can better understand it. Tell them you are confident that we all understand 10 (or 10^1) and 100 (or 10^2), but as numbers get very large or very small, it is harder to make sense of them. The video gives an idea of our limits—some of the numbers it explores are so large, they go beyond our solar system, and we are unlikely to ever encounter them. But other numbers, such as 10,000 (or 10^4) or 1,000,000 (or 10^6) or $\frac{1}{10,000}$, we might find in our world. You might ask students when they have heard these numbers used, give them a chance to turn and talk, and then share examples. Then tell students that the question they will work to answer today is, What do very large and very small numbers look like?

Tell students that the class will be creating a Museum of the Very Large and Small. Each group will get to choose a power of 10—a number made by multiplying or dividing 1 repeatedly by 10—and construct a museum exhibit to show others what this number means. Show students the materials they will have access to for the construction of their exhibit, and tell them who their audience will be.

Explore

Students work in small groups to choose a power of 10 to explore, either a very large or very small number. Each group does not need to select a unique number, but a variety of values across the class will lead to a more interesting museum. Ask students to find multiple ways to represent what that number means so that they can teach others.

Students create an exhibit for a class museum that will help others understand the meaning of this number in the same way we all understand 10 or 100. Provide students with materials for exploring and constructing their exhibits, such as posters, bulletin boards, cardboard boxes, tape, scissors, colored paper, and markers. Students may want to use manipulatives, such as base 10 blocks, unifix cubes, or tiles, to make models of their number, or measuring tools such as meter sticks, if students would like to model using distance. Students might draw pictures or diagrams, use words, or collect objects to help them make their number clear to their audience. Students might also want access to cameras or other technology to capture their number. For instance, some students might be inspired by the Eames's video and want to create their own video for their exhibit.

Present

Stage your Museum of the Very Large and Small by putting up the student-created exhibits around your classroom or school hallway. Consider how you want to arrange them in your space. You may want to array them from smallest to largest for visitors. We encourage you to invite, if possible, other classes, teachers, or families to your exhibition opening. At least one member of each group should stand by the group's exhibit to answer questions and explain.

Provide all visitors (your students included) with sticky notes. Ask visitors to jot two different kinds of comments on their stickies as they move around the museum: "I'm surprised that . . ." and "I wonder . . ." Create a chart or spot on a wall for visitors to post each kind of observation, with one area labeled "I'm surprised that . . ." and one labeled "I wonder . . ."

Discuss

After everyone has had the chance to see the exhibits and any classroom visitors have gone, convene your class to discuss the museum. Mix students into small groups for table discussion, and ask them to discuss the following questions:

- What did you learn from making your exhibit?
- What did you learn from the other exhibits?

Ask some students to share what their tables discussed. Then ask students to gather near the banks of sticky notes. Discuss the following:

- Look at what people wrote that surprised them. What patterns do you notice? What did our visitors learn?
- Look at what people were wondering. What kinds of questions were visitors still thinking about? What are the most intriguing questions? What might be worth exploring?

Extend

Some of your visitors may have posed interesting questions worthy of further investigation. Consider spending time as a class pursuing the most compelling of these questions.

Look-Fors

- **Are students focusing on the meaning of the numbers first?** Before students can construct an exhibit, they need to explore the meaning of the number their group has chosen and to find interesting, creative, and effective ways to represent it. Encourage students to brainstorm many ways and select the representations or explanations that they think are the most vivid, surprising, or useful.
- **Are students being clear about units?** The numbers have meaning only when we define what units we are using. For instance, 1,000,000 looks different when the unit is a person, a minute, a grain of rice, or a centimeter. Students should use several units to make the meaning of their number clear, just as we all understand 100 more when we consider 100 people, minutes, grains of rice, or centimeters. Depending on the size of the number they are exploring, students may want to make the units they use larger or smaller. For instance, it is easier to imagine 1,000,000 with grains of rice than with miles; it is easier to consider $\frac{1}{10,000}$ when the unit is the length of the hallway than when it is a unifix cube.
- **Are students using what they know about more familiar powers of 10 to build understanding of their larger and small numbers?** Students choosing

10,000, for instance, should be able to think about what they know about 1,000 and make that 10 times larger as an entry point for solving. Support students in starting with a unit and progressively making it 10 times larger or $\frac{1}{10}$ the size, again and again.

- **How are students communicating their findings?** Students sometimes struggle to imagine the perspectives of others. In constructing an exhibit, students will need to think about how to communicate what their number means to someone who may not have considered it before. Students should be planning both for what to show—with objects, models, pictures, or diagrams—and what to tell—with labels, title, captions, or signs.

Reflect

What did you learn from the museum that you think will be most useful to you in the future? Why?

Using Numbers and Symbols Flexibly

One of the most important mindsets any student of mathematics can have is that of an investigator—someone who is willing to play with ideas and approach mathematics as a flexible subject. When I studied two groups of students in England who went through different school approaches, one that was traditional and one that was project based (see Boaler, 2002), the students from the project-based school learned that they could solve any problem, using the flexible tools they had learned. They approached mathematical situations, as students and later as adults (see Boaler & Selling, 2017), as problems to be solved, and they were willing to try different approaches. The students who had learned with the traditional approach thought they had to remember a set method, and would give up when situations did not look like the math questions they remembered from class. These different mindsets and approaches to mathematics gave the students from the two schools different approaches to their jobs and lives, and the students who had learned to flexibly use mathematics went on to greater success in their lives (Boaler & Selling, 2017).

Mathematical flexibility is a wonderful approach to have, and one that we encourage in this big idea. We do so by showing students that numbers can exist in many different forms—as squares in a diagram, in expressions, in a famous triangle, and through creations they make when they combine numbers.

Steve Strogatz is a mathematician at Cornell whom we feature on youcubed.org as he teaches mathematics as a creative investigative subject to undergraduates. Steve is the author of many books that show the beauty and creativity in mathematics, and he, like us, is frustrated that mathematics is so misrepresented in many schools. I include interviews with Steve in my Mathematical Mindsets online class (https://tinyurl.com/mathematicalmindsetcourse); the following is a quotation from one of the interviews with Steve: "Rigor is the overemphasized part of math—at the expense of creativity and ingenuity and intuition. I mean, it's shocking to me that people don't see math as creative, though I understand why not. The way we teach it, tend to teach it in elementary school, K to 12, and even in college does not tend to emphasize creativity, to put it mildly. That is, you're taught that you should follow the rules; you must use precise definitions."

In Steve's teaching at Cornell, which you can see at www.youcubed.org/higher-ed/, he emphasizes the creativity and intuition that are so central to good mathematical thinking. In the set of activities for this big idea, we also encourage intuition and creativity, while at the same time introducing and allowing formal mathematical representations, to show that mathematics is a blend of the formal and informal.

In our Visualize activity, we would like you to introduce students to a number pattern using a number talk approach. If you have not used or seen a visual, dot-card number talk, you can see me teaching sixth graders using that approach here: www.youcubed.org/jo-dot-card-number-talk/. The task is for students to work out different ways to represent the image using multiple expressions and grouping symbols as needed. We recommend that students color-code their solutions to show connections. Color coding, as I wrote in the introduction to this book, is a really worthwhile activity in mathematics, helping students see the connections that are critical to mathematics. We ask students to find different ways of representing either the picture with expressions or the expression with pictures, which will encourage creativity, and to show the connections through color coding.

In our Play activity, students will be given time to explore a wonderful mathematical creation: Pascal's Triangle. In our work with students, they have been fascinated and enthralled by this famous triangle. We ask students to first explore the patterns they see in the triangle and then to try different numbers in the triangle to see what happens. This is another opportunity to ask students to color-code their results. We also pose some discussion questions and ask students to come up with their own conjectures and theories about the famous triangle.

In our Investigate activity, we give students a problem that is like the "four 4s problem" that we share on youcubed.org, except that they work with the numbers 1, 2, 4, and 9. As with the four 4s problem, they can use the numbers in any way, with any expressions, to try to find all the values from, in this case, 1 to 100. This will create a nice opportunity for some specialized notation. Exponents (using one of the digits), square roots (note that 1, 4, and 9 are squares), and factorial (!) are all needed if all the numbers are to be found. Factorial is a mathematical operation that is not usually taught in fifth grade, but it is totally accessible for fifth graders, and we have found young children to be fascinated by factorial. Students will be more engaged when you show it to them, and their brains will be more primed to learn it, if they first encounter a need for the method. Mathematics classrooms typically teach methods to students before they encounter any need to use them, which causes students to be bored and to think "When will I ever need this?" A really interesting research study (Schwartz & Bransford, 1998) showed that students learned more when they worked, using their intuition, on problems that needed methods, before they learned the methods. They did not learn the methods until they had encountered a need for them. This caused the students' brains to be primed to learn them. In our teaching of four 4s, we leave students to realize that some numbers are unfound, before we teach factorial to them. They are then really excited to use it and continue to be excited about the factorial operation for a long time.

Jo Boaler

Seeing Expressions

Snapshot

Grouping symbols are introduced in this visual task, where students learn to represent groups of squares with expressions. Partners work on creating multiple ways to match images to expressions and color-code the connections between them.

Connection to CCSS
5.OA.1
5.OA.2

Agenda

Activity	Time	Description/Prompt	Materials
Launch	15 min	Introduce students to representing expressions with grouping symbols through a visual number talk.	• Seeing Expressions Number Image, for display (projected, on a chart, or copied from the provided template) • Colored markers
Explore	30+ min	Partners work on representing an image with multiple expressions, using grouping symbols as needed. Then partners choose additional tasks from a task bank of two images and two expressions. Students color-code their solutions to show connections.	• Seeing Expressions Tasks 1, 2, 3, and 4, a copy of each sheet for each partnership • Colors
Discuss	15–20 min	Share the expressions and images student created. Discuss when grouping symbols were useful and the challenges of creating images for expressions.	Space to post solutions
Extend	30+ min	Partners create and road-test their own puzzles, starting with either an image or an expression. Then partnerships can swap with one another and try out puzzles created by other groups.	Paper and colors

To the Teacher

This lesson may be students' first introduction to grouping symbols in expressions. The initial number talk is a critical opportunity for you to model how to use these symbols conventionally as you record students' thinking in expressions. We encourage you to try the number talk task yourself to see how decomposing the image in different ways changes the expression you might write. This will help you anticipate what students might say and what expressions you might need to record as they explain their thinking.

We also think that color coding is a powerful strategy for showing connections, and have used it throughout this lesson. If students have not had exposure to this tool for representing thinking, then you will want to make this technique more explicit in the launch and encourage students to try it out as they work. You may want to remind students that it is important to exercise different brain pathways, and that when we see things in different ways—in numbers and images, for example—this encourages brain crossing.

Activity

Launch

Launch this activity by presenting students with the image here of squares grouped in interesting ways, and, in the style of a number talk, conduct a discussion of how many there are. If you don't use visual number talks, or know what they are, you can see Jo teach one here: www.youcubed.org/jo-dot-card-number-talk/. Ask students to figure out how many there are without counting them all individually. Ask students to pay attention to how they see them, and to signal with a thumbs-up when they are ready. After students have had a minute or two to think about this task and are signaling that they are ready to talk, ask them how many they saw and how they saw them.

As students report how they saw the total number of squares, you'll want to be careful about how you record what they say. You'll want to do two kinds of recording. First, you'll mark up the picture to indicate the different ways the student decomposed the picture into groups. We encourage you to color-code the picture to show the different parts the student used. You may want to have multiple copies of this cluster of squares so that you can mark each one up for each way students saw the squares grouped. Here's an example of marking up the diagram when the student saw a group that was 5 × 2 with 2 more on top, then saw that there were three of these groups:

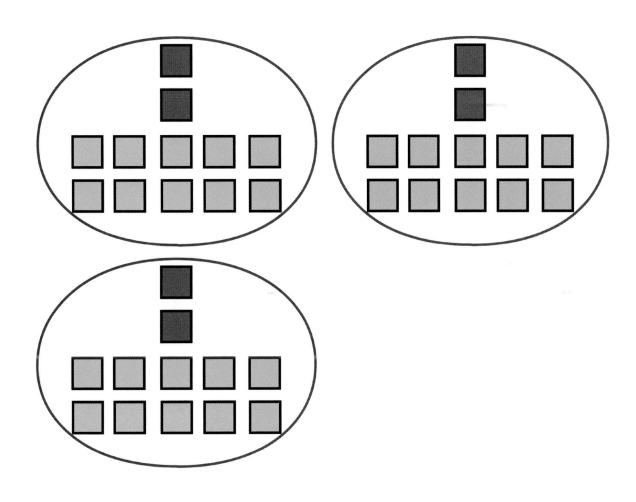

Second, you'll record the mathematical thinking the student did to find the quantities, using an expression that uses grouping symbols in an algebraically accurate way. If possible, we encourage you to color-code this expression using the same colors you used for grouping the picture. This will enable students to see how the groups of squares become grouped algebraically. Here is an example of how you could record the expression for the image, using colors to show how they are related:

$$(5 \times 2 + 2) \times 3$$

Introduce the activity for the day. Students will have a choice of four tasks. Two are images like the one the class just did together, and two are expressions like the ones you wrote for the picture. Ask students to try an image task first and then choose any one from the remaining three. Challenge students to find multiple ways of representing either the picture with expressions or the expression with pictures, color-coding them to show how they connect.

Explore

Ask student partnerships to choose one of the two image tasks to start with. You will need copies of the tasks so that partners can complete more than one during this exploration time. For each image task, ask students to first try to describe what it is they see, putting in words how they see the quantities. Students do this aloud with their partner, just as they would explain it to the class in a number talk. Then students record in words what they see in that column of their sheet. Finally, students use what they see and their description to create an expression to represent the total number of squares in the image that matches how they saw it. Challenge students to group the clusters of squares in different ways to see what expressions they create and to find as many different ways as they can to represent the image.

For each expression task, students examine the expression and try to imagine what the expression could be showing. Partners talk about this and then record what they imagine the image could look like from the expression. Then students try to create the image that could match what they see in the expression. Encourage students to reimagine the expression in as many different ways as they can.

For all tasks, ask students to color-code their work to show the relationship between the image and the expression.

Discuss

You may want to debrief each task, one by one, by having students share different expressions or images they created. Alternatively, you might ask partners to share the image or expression they created that they are most proud of or that they think is the most creative, interesting solution. In some form, you will want to ask, What did we come up with? You may also want to discuss what the solutions for each task have in common.

After an opportunity to share solutions, ask some overarching questions to help students think across the tasks:

- When were the grouping symbols useful? What ways of decomposing the figures led to the need for grouping symbols? Which didn't?
- How did you tackle moving in the opposite direction—creating pictures for an expression? What was different about it? How did you have to think differently?

Extend

Ask partners to make their own picture or expression and then find multiple ways to represent the picture or expression they created. You might challenge students to come up with a puzzle that would be interesting for someone else to solve, and after they have had a chance to test it out, have partnerships swap puzzles with each other. You can post the most interesting puzzles and solutions, and ask students to nominate puzzles or solutions that are creative or intriguing.

Look-Fors

- **Are students using grouping symbols accurately?** If this is students' first exposure to their use, they may under- or overuse them. Provide some guidance about how to reason through when and where symbols are needed and when they are redundant.
- **Are students color-coding?** If this is a new strategy, students may struggle to reflect on how to use color to show connections. It may help many students to do their initial thinking in pencil and then add color.
- **Are students finding multiple ways to represent each task?** Students might see one or two ways easily, but need encouragement to think beyond what came initially to mind.

Reflect

What are grouping symbols useful for? How do they change the meaning of an expression?

Mindset Mathematics, Grade 5, copyright © 2018 by Jo Boaler, Jen Munson, Cathy Williams. Reproduced by permission of John Wiley & Sons, Inc.

Seeing Expressions Task 1

How do you see it?

Pattern	I see (draw and color it)	Imagine (write an expression)

Seeing Expressions Task 2

How do you see it?

Pattern	I see (draw and color it)	Imagine (write an expression)

Mindset Mathematics, Grade 5, copyright © 2018 by Jo Boaler, Jen Munson, Cathy Williams.
Reproduced by permission of John Wiley & Sons, Inc.

Seeing Expressions Task 3

How do you see it?

Pattern	I see (draw and color it)	Imagine (write an expression)
		$4 \times (2 + 4) \times 3$
		$4 \times (2 + 4) \times 3$
		$4 \times (2 + 4) \times 3$

Mindset Mathematics, Grade 5, copyright © 2018 by Jo Boaler, Jen Munson, Cathy Williams.
Reproduced by permission of John Wiley & Sons, Inc.

259

Seeing Expressions Task 4

How do you see it?

Pattern	I see (draw and color it)	Imagine (write an expression)
		$(5 + 5 + 2) \times 5$
		$(5 + 5 + 2) \times 5$
		$(5 + 5 + 2) \times 5$

Inside Pascal's Triangle

Snapshot

In this activity, we play with the patterns in Pascal's Triangle, representing them with expressions. We play with the starting number of Pascal's Triangle to see how it changes the row sums and their expressions.

Connection to CCSS
5.OA.1
5.OA.2

Agenda

Activity	Time	Description/Prompt	Materials
Launch	5 min	Show students Pascal's Triangle and tell them that there is a pattern to how it is constructed.	Pascal's Triangle sheet, for display (on a projector or by other means)
Explore	20+ min	Students work in partners to try to find the pattern that governs Pascal's Triangle and to use that pattern to find missing values. Students then look for additional patterns in the triangle, color-coding what they have found.	• Pascal's Triangle sheet, multiple copies per student • Colors
Discuss	10 min	Discuss the pattern that creates the triangle and the other patterns students discovered.	
Explore	30+ min	Students investigate patterns in the row sums of Pascal's Triangle, writing efficient expressions for finding the sums. Students investigate whether these patterns remain the same if the starting number of the triangle is changed.	Your Pascal's Triangle sheet, at least two per student
Discuss	15 min	Discuss how to write efficient expressions for the row sums. Then discuss the patterns in the row sums for the first Pascal's Triangle and for those with new starting numbers. Does the pattern hold?	

To the Teacher

Pascal's Triangle is a famous two-dimensional pattern of numbers arrayed in a triangular formation. At the top of the triangle is the number 1. Each number below is the sum of the two numbers above it.

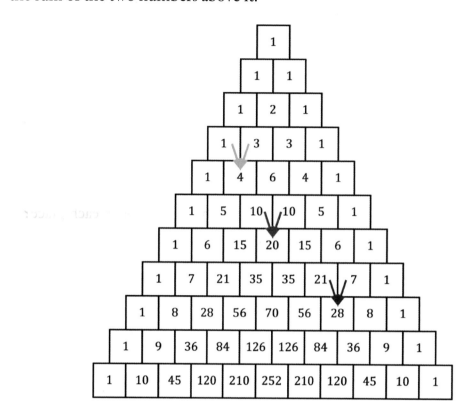

There are many patterns inside Pascal's Triangle—so many, in fact, that mathematicians believe that all the patterns have not yet been discovered. Patterns exist moving across, down, and within the triangle. You might discover interesting things in the triangle by looking at different kinds of numbers, such as odds or primes. Some of these patterns become clear only when the triangle is quite large—one reason that there is more to discover in Pascal's Triangle. In this puzzle, you'll want to encourage students to be inquisitive about the triangle, to try a hunch, and to simply ask, What would happen if . . .? We encourage you to investigate what patterns you notice in Pascal's Triangle by trying this activity yourself or, even better, with a group of teacher colleagues. We think you'll find this intriguing and even more engaging to teach if you explore first yourself.

Because of the many avenues for puzzling and exploration in this activity, the lesson may be spread across multiple days. Follow your students' curiosity and give them the time they need.

Mindset Mathematics, Grade 5

Activity

Launch

Start by showing students the image of Pascal's Triangle provided, which has some missing numbers. Tell students that this is a famous pattern of numbers called Pascal's triangle, which has been found to have connections to lots of other math ideas. The triangle contains many patterns and can grow bigger and bigger following those patterns. There is a pattern to how to build this particular triangle. Ask, Can you find the pattern that builds the triangle so that you can fill in the blanks?

Explore

Ask students to work with a partner to find the patterns in Pascal's triangle that help them find the missing values. Each person should have their own copy of the triangle to look at closely. Ask, How can you predict what number should be in each place?

Once students have figured out the pattern that builds Pascal's Triangle and they have completed their own, they then look for other patterns in the triangle. Ask students to color-code or mark up the triangle to show the patterns they've found. If students get stuck, you might prompt them to explore types of numbers, such as even and odds, or to look for patterns in the arrangement of the numbers, such as diagonals.

Discuss

First debrief the central pattern in Pascal's Triangle that enables you to predict what value will go in each position. You might ask the following:

- What patterns did you find that helped you find the missing values?
- How is Pascal's Triangle built?

Then ask students to share their findings around other patterns. You will want some way of showing these patterns on the triangle. You might have students present their triangles, with their color coding, on a document camera or simply hold them up for others to see. You might decide to make a display of these different patterns, grouping them to show relationships. You might also decide to show the patterns by color-coding your own class triangle on a large piece of chart paper. Determine the way to share the patterns students found that is most suitable for your context.

Explore

Let's explore the row sums, or the total value of the numbers in one row of the triangle. What patterns exist in the row sums? Ask students to write expressions for finding the sum of the values in each row. Although students certainly could simply write an expression that lists the numbers in order with addition signs, there are other, more efficient ways to find the row sums. Encourage students to try to find efficient expressions.

Once students have explored how to write efficient expressions for the row sums and looked for patterns, ask them whether they think the pattern they found will be the same if the triangle started with a number different than 1. Give students copies of Your Pascal's Triangle and ask them to choose a new single-digit starting number to see what happens to the row-sum pattern. Again, ask students to write expressions for the row sums as they work. Ask, What changed in your new triangle? What didn't? Why?

Students may want to create yet another triangle to see whether the patterns they've observed so far continue with other starting values. Ask, Did your pattern hold? Or do you want to revise your thinking about the row-sum patterns?

Discuss

Start the discussion by asking students to share what they found in the row sums of Pascal's Triangle:

- What expressions did you find to represent row sums?
- What ways did you find to make the expressions efficient?

Then ask students to discuss their various findings from changing the starting number. Across the class, students probably accumulated lots of evidence that is more powerful and interesting when put together. Be sure to use the power of many examples to make students' pattern ideas and predictions more precise.

- How did the row sums change when the starting number changed? What didn't change?
- What theories did you come up with for how they changed and why?
- What do you think would happen if we started Pascal's Triangle with a larger number? What evidence is there from our work today to support your prediction?

Look-Fors

- **Are students' triangles accurate?** We have found that students can struggle to see the pattern in the triangle and to apply it across the missing values. This is a good time to remind students that struggle is really important, that it is a time when our brains are most active and growing. The blanks in the triangle were placed strategically in locations where some students run into trouble. Help students think about what rule they have found for the pattern and how to apply it to all spaces in the triangle. This will become even more challenging when students create their own triangles from scratch. You might encourage students in the partnership to each create their own triangle with the same starting number so that they can check each other as they go.

- **Are students writing efficient expressions for finding the row sums?** Students can certainly find the row sum by adding $1 + 3 + 3 + 1$, but the symmetry of the triangle should help students see that they could write an equivalent expression, such as $2 \times (1 + 3)$. You might prompt students to think about the first activity in this big idea and draw each value as dots or squares to help them literally see ways to group that would be useful.

- **Are students struggling to think about patterns across patterns?** The patterns we are talking about in the row sums are nested, in that first we look at the pattern of Pascal's Triangle, then we sum the rows and look for a new pattern created out of the triangle, and then finally we look for patterns across the row sums of different triangles. This can get dizzying for students. Keeping triangles well labeled and posting them side by side during the discussion can help students think across the triangles. If students in their partner work are getting lost, you might ask them: How can we organize your thinking in each part to make it clearer for you? What labels would be helpful? How could color be helpful?

Reflect

How did writing efficient expressions make the patterns in the row sums clearer?

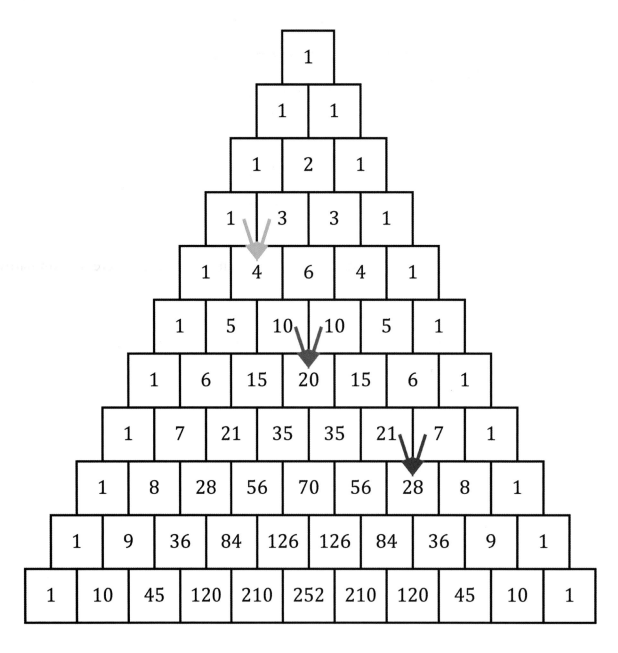

 **Your Pascal's Triangle**

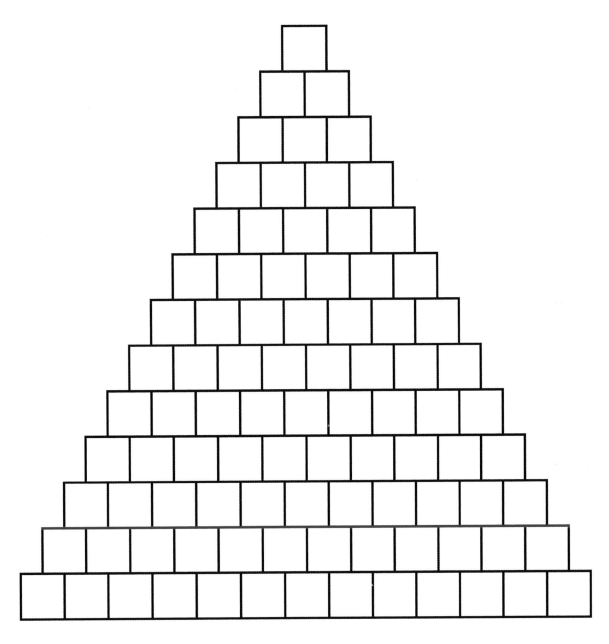

The 1492 Problem

Snapshot

Students investigate how they might use the digits in the number 1492 and mathematical symbols to write expressions for each value from 1 to 100. The class collects expressions as a group to determine whether or not it is possible. Students may be introduced to some new notation they can use as tools in their investigation: exponents, square roots, and factorial.

Connection to CCSS
5.OA.1
5.OA.2

Agenda

Activity	Time	Description/Prompt	Materials
Launch	10–15 min	Ask students to use all four numbers 1, 4, 9, and 2 and any mathematical symbols to create an expression. What values can you create? Introduce the investigation and how students can record their thinking.	Class collection chart
Explore	30–45 min (each day)	Students use the numbers 1, 4, 9, and 2 and mathematical symbols to create expressions for every value from 1 to 100. The class collects expressions on a shared chart or display.	• Class collection chart and markers • The five 1492 Problem recording sheets, one packet per student
Discuss	10 min	Students discuss the strategies they have developed, the values found and still missing, and, possibly, new notation tools they might use to find missing values.	Class collection chart
Extend	Ongoing	After the class has whittled the list of values down to a few stubborn "Most Wanted" values, the chart remains up so that students can continue to explore on their own time.	Class collection chart or "Most Wanted" chart

To the Teacher

This investigation will take at least two days of class time, as well as a more extended period for students to continue to look for additional solutions. In our experience, this is an investigation that students linger on, puzzling over the last few elusive values for days after the class ends its full-time exploration. We suggest that you make a large class recording space (on butcher paper, a bulletin board, or a series of posters) and leave it up for as long as students are still engaged in pursuing missing values.

In order for students to find all the values from 1 to 100, they will need to use the numbers 1, 4, 9, and 2 (and no others), operation symbols, grouping symbols, and three more specialized forms of notation: exponents (using one of the digits), square roots (note that 1, 4, and 9 are squares), and factorial (!). Factorial is not commonly used in elementary school mathematics, but is an operation that we find students are excited to use. Placing the factorial symbol after a number indicates that the number should be multiplied by every counting number smaller than itself. Thus:

$$4! = 4 \times 3 \times 2 \times 1$$
$$9! = 9 \times 8 \times 7 \times 6 \times 5 \times 4 \times 3 \times 2 \times 1$$

Factorial is simply a specialized multiplication operation, which students will enjoy exploring. We encourage you to look for good moments to introduce these new ideas to students in this investigation based on what they have already had experience with and where they are in the activity. Often, we find that on the first day of the investigation, students have plenty to do generating expressions with familiar operations. Indeed, most of the values from 1 to 100 can be made with familiar operations. As students start to whittle down the list of missing values, you will want to offer them some symbolic tools to open up their exploration. You might choose to launch the second (or third) day of the investigation by introducing these to the whole class, or use the discussion at the end of the first day as a place to offer these new tools.

Activity

Launch

Introduce the task by asking what values you can make with the numbers 1, 4, 9, and 2 and any operation by writing an accurate expression. Be sure to record these numbers in a shared place for students to see—on a whiteboard, chart, or projector. Tell them they can use any mathematical symbols they can think of, including operation and grouping symbols, provided that they use them accurately. Approach the launch of this task as a number talk. Give students a moment to think privately, then ask for values and record them. Then ask for a couple of students to defend an answer by giving their expression. Record the expression, being careful about notation and asking any clarifying questions necessary. Ask the class whether they agree or disagree that the offered expression equals the value the student is defending, and have them explain their reasoning.

After students have defended at least two values accurately and the class agrees that the expressions match the values, introduce the activity. The goal of this investigation is to use the numbers 1, 4, 9, and 2 and mathematical operations to make every value from 1 to 100. Is it possible? The class will be working collectively to find all the values; point out that they have already found two. Ask students to record the expressions they find in two places: their own recording sheet and a class record chart. They might find that there is even more than one expression that creates the same value. They should add these to the class record chart, too, so that they can see *all* the ways the class has come up with during the investigation.

Explore

Can you make every value from 1 to 100 using numbers 1, 4, 9, and 2 and mathematical symbols? Students are encouraged to talk and work together, but we recommend that each student get their own sheet with the numbers 1 to 100 printed for them to record their own expressions. Post a large sheet of butcher paper similarly labeled for students to contribute to the class solutions. When students find more than one way to make the same answer, make sure they record those multiple solutions.

As students explore, encourage them to check each other and to ask for others to check their work. Students may find that they have a great idea but that they need to revise the symbols they are using to convey that idea. Having another person check their expressions is a great way to catch areas for revision. If any students need a break from searching for their own expressions, you may want to have them serve in a checking role for the class collection chart, working each expression to confirm that it yields the stated value. This is a needed and valuable role for students to play, giving them experience evaluating expressions, in addition to their work creating them.

Discuss

When students get stuck or have worked for a full day, pull them together to discuss what strategies have been useful. Ask, How have you been generating expressions? Students might offer strategies for taking one expression and modifying it to get several new ones, or strategies for searching for a particular value.

Look over the class collection chart and ask the class to reflect on what they have found and not yet found.

- Why do you think that some values were found quickly, while there are others that no one has found?
- Are there any values with more than one expression? Why do you think that is?
- Did you find any expressions that did not work? Or any places you needed to revise? What helped you catch those mistakes?

To find solutions for all of the answers, students will need some additional forms of notation: exponents (using 1, 2, 4, or 9), square root, and factorial. You might use the discussion as an opportunity to introduce one or all of these if students seem hungry for more tools. Alternatively, you could launch the second (or third) day of investigation by introducing one or more of these tools. When launching the second day, be sure to draw students' attention to the values that the class is still collectively searching for. Students can choose to focus on those or on finding ones that they themselves have not yet found.

Extend

After students have had a couple of days to work on generating expressions and the list of values from 1 to 100 has been whittled down, post a list of the "Most Wanted" values—those that still have not been found—for kids to continue to look for in their spare moments (on the bus is a popular time!). Alternatively, you can highlight or block these values off on your class chart so that they are prominent.

The class can also discuss lingering questions about what they have found:

- Which answers have the most solutions? Which have only one? Are there any that have no solution? Why do you think that is?
- How close do you think we are to having found all that are possible? Why?

Look-Fors

- **Are students using operations and notation accurately?** Perhaps the biggest stretch in this work is using operations accurately in the language of mathematics. Employing this language requires careful thought and practice, which this investigation is intended to support. Encourage students to check expressions for each other, and, even more productively, to ask others to check their work. Prompt students to explain when they disagree and to support each other in making revisions. It is important that this activity keep a tone of joint effort, rather than one of competition between students.

- **Are students ready for new forms of notation?** When students have found half or more of the expressions and appear hungry (even frustrated) searching for more, they may be ready for one or more of the additional forms of notation used in this problem. It is important that students are eager in the midst of the investigation, rather than overwhelmed at the beginning. Students are far more likely to make meaningful (and accurate) use of these symbols if they are starting to run out of possibilities with the familiar symbols.

Reflect

What operations are most useful and flexible? Why? When are the less common operations useful? Why?

References

Boaler, J. (2002). *Experiencing school mathematics: Traditional and reform approaches to teaching and their impact on student learning.*: Mahwah, NJ: Erlbaum.

Boaler, J., & Selling, S. (2017). Psychological imprisonment or intellectual freedom? A longitudinal study of contrasting school mathematics approaches and their impact on adults' lives. *Journal of Research in Mathematics Education, 48*(1), 78–105.

Schwartz, D., & Bransford, J. (1998). A time for telling. *Cognition and Instruction, 16,* 475–522.

The 1492 Problem

1	11
2	12
3	13
4	14
5	15
6	16
7	17
8	18
9	19
10	20

The 1492 Problem

21	31
22	32
23	33
24	34
25	35
26	36
27	37
28	38
29	39
30	40

The 1492 Problem

41	51
42	52
43	53
44	54
45	55
46	56
47	57
48	58
49	59
50	60

61	71
62	72
63	73
64	74
65	75
66	76
67	77
68	78
69	79
70	80

The 1492 Problem

81	91
82	92
83	93
84	94
85	95
86	96
87	97
88	98
89	99
90	100

Appendix

Centimeter Dot Paper

Appendix

Isometric Dot Paper

About the Authors

Dr. Jo Boaler is a professor of mathematics education at Stanford University, and the cofounder of Youcubed. She is the author of the first MOOC on mathematics teaching and learning. Former roles have included being the Marie Curie Professor of Mathematics Education in England, a mathematics teacher in London comprehensive schools, and a lecturer and researcher at King's College, London. Her work has been published in the *Times,* the *Telegraph,* the *Wall Street Journal,* and many other news outlets. The BBC recently named Jo one of the eight educators "changing the face of education."

Jen Munson is a doctoral candidate at Stanford University, a professional developer, and a former classroom teacher. Her doctoral research focuses on how coaching can support teachers in growing their mathematics instructional practices, particularly in the elementary grades, and how teacher-student interactions influence equitable math learning. As a professional developer, she focuses on growing teachers' and leaders' capacity to craft rich, responsive, and equitable mathematics classrooms. Before leaving the classroom to coach, she taught elementary and middle school in Washington, DC, Chicago, and the Seattle area.

Cathy Williams is the cofounder and director of Youcubed. She completed an applied mathematics major at University of California, San Diego before becoming a high school math teacher for 18 years in San Diego County. After teaching, she became a county office coordinator and then district mathematics director. As part of her leadership work, Cathy has designed professional development and curriculum. Her district work in the Vista Unified School District won a California Golden Bell for instruction in 2013 for the K–12 Innovation Cohort in mathematics. In Vista, Cathy worked with Jo changing the way mathematics was taught across the district.

Acknowledgments

We thank Jill Marsal, our book agent. We are also very grateful to our Youcubed army of teachers. Thanks to Robin Anderson for drawing the network diagram on our cover. Finally, we thank our children—and dogs!—for putting up with our absences from family life as we worked to bring our vision of mathematical mindset tasks to life.

Index

A Box of Boxes: addition and, 45, 48; agenda for, 44–45; color coding in, 46, 49; comprehension questions for, 49; dimensions in, 44, 46, 47, 48, 51; discussion in, 44, 45, 47, 48–49; exploration in, 44, 45, 46–47, 48; language of mathematics in, 46; launching, 44, 45, 46; sheets for, 44, 45, 46, 48, 50–51; volume in, 24, 44, 45, 46, 47, 48, 49, 51

Brain: connections in, 23–24, 144, 170–171, 200, 251; growth of, 14, 38, 49, 54, 82, 171, 265; networks for mental arithmetic, 10; priming, 249; science of, 2, 3, 5, 10–11, 14, 23

Brainstorming, 17, 104, 120, 202, 205, 244

Brownie Pan Template, 172, 175, 179

Building norms, 17–21

Burton, Leone, 8

C

Cards. *See* Creating Cards

China, 199

City of Cubes, 23; agenda for, 33–34; Architectural Drawings sheets for, 33, 35, 39–40; color coding in, 33, 34, 36, 37; comprehension questions for, 38; discussion in, 33, 34, 36–37; launching, 33, 35, 36; Play agenda in, 33, 34, 36, 37; Puzzle sheet for, 33, 36, 38, 41–43; volume in, 33, 37

"Cockcroft Report," 53

Color: in Make a Fake activity, 94, 95, 96, 97, 98, 100; in Picking Paintings Apart activity, 83, 84, 85, 86; in Squares with a Difference activity, 101, 102, 104, 105, 108–109

Color coding: in The 1492 Problem activity, 248, 261, 263, 265; for addition, 6, 7; in A Box of Boxes activity, 46, 49; of Coordinate

Plane, 115–116, 133, 134, 136, 138; in Cube of Cubes activity, 33, 34, 36, 37; in Fraction Blizzard activity, 182, 185; in Pattern Carnival activity, 154, 158; in Seeing Expressions, 250–260; in Seeing Growth on a Graph activity, 162; in Solids, Inside and out activity, 28; in Squares with a Difference activity, 82; in Table Patterns activity, 133, 134, 138; in Two-Pattern Tango activity, 144, 145, 146, 147; in Wondering with Fractions activity, 67, 70

Committee of Inquiry into the Teaching of Mathematics in Schools, 53

Common Core, 9

Common denominators: in Make a Fake activity, 95; in Picking Paintings Apart activity, 83, 84, 86

Composition II in Red, Blue, and Yellow, 92, 93

Comprehension questions: for A Box of Boxes, 49; for City of Cubes, 38; for Creating Cards, 205–206; for Cuisenaire Trains, 213–214; for Filling Small and Large, 238; for The 1492 Problem, 272; for Fraction Blizzard, 65–66; for Fraction Division Conundrum, 221–222; for Fractions in a Pan, 177–178; for Getting around the Plane, 121–122; for Inside Pascal's Triangle, 265; for Make a Fake, 97–98; for Making Snowflakes, 60; for Museum of the Very Large and Small, 244–245; for Pattern Carnival, 157–158; for Picking Paintings Apart, 86–87; for Pieces and Parts, 184–185; for Seeing Expressions, 255; for Seeing Growth on a Graph, 164; for Ship Shape, 128; for Solids, Inside

and Out, 29–30; for Squares with a Difference, 108–110; for The Sum of the Parts, 191–192; for Table Patterns, 137–139; for Two-Pattern Tango, 148–149; for The Unit You, 230–231; for Wondering with Fractions, 71–72

Conceptual compression, 5

Conceptual engagement: memorization contrasted with, 4–5; Visualize activities and, 11. *See also* Big Ideas, overviews of

Conjectures, 220

Connecting patterns, 143–167

Convincing, learning to be, 8; Paper Folding activity for, 19–21

Coordinate graphs, 115–116, 144, 159

Coordinate plane, 115–117; sheets for, 133, 136, 141

Coordinate plane Investigate activity. *See* Table Patterns

Coordinate plane Play activity. *See* Ship Shape

Coordinate plane Visualize activity. *See* Getting around the Plane

Cordero, Montse, 1

Could, 176

Creating Cards, 200, 201, 203, 204, 207–208; agenda for, 201–202; comprehension questions for, 205–206; discussion in, 201, 202, 203–204, 205, 206; exploration in, 201, 203, 204, 205; intuition in, 202; launching, 201, 203; number sentences in, 201, 203–204, 205–206; recording chart for, 204, 205; Recording Sheet, 201, 204, 208

Creativity, 15, 54, 71, 143, 147, 247–248; Investigate activities and, 14; Play activities and, 13; Visualize activities and, 12

Cubes, 23–24

Cubes Investigate activity. *See* A Box of Boxes

Cubes Play activity. *See* City of Cubes

Cubes Visualize activity. *See* Solids, Inside and Out

Cuisenaire Trains, 200, 209–216; addition in, 214; agenda for, 209–210; comprehension questions for, 213–214; Cuisenaire Train image for, 211, 215; discussion in, 209, 211, 213; launching, 209, 210, 211, 212; number sentences in, 213–214; partitioning in, 210, 211, 212, 213, 216; Play agenda in, 209, 212; struggle in, 214

Curriculum standards, 9

D

Data points, 119, 120, 121

Denominators: common, 83, 84, 86, 95; fraction equivalence, numerators and, 81–82; in fraction multiplication, 169, 177; in Make a Fake activity, 95, 98; in Picking Paintings Apart activity, 83, 84, 86

Desmos, 116

Difference, 102, 108

Dimensional representations, two- and three-: in City of Cubes activity, 33, 34, 38–43; in Filling Small and Large activity, 238; in Solids, Inside and Out activity, 23, 25, 26–27, 28, 30, 31, 32; struggles with, 26, 30, 34, 38

Dimensions: in A Box of Boxes activity, 44, 46, 47, 48, 51; Coordinate Plane and, 115; in Coordinate Plane Visualize activity, 118, 119, 120, 121–122; of Little Boxes, 51; of Packing Boxes, 51; of Pascal's Triangle, 262

Discussion: A Box of Boxes for, 44, 45, 47, 48–49; City of Cubes for, 33, 34, 36–37; Creating Cards for, 201, 202, 203–204, 205, 206; Cuisenaire Trains for,

209, 211, 213; Filling Small and Large for, 234, 237; The 1492 Problem for, 268, 269, 271, 272; Fraction Blizzard for, 54, 62, 64–65, 66; Fraction Division Conundrum for, 217, 218, 219, 220–221; Fractions in a Pan for, 172, 173, 174, 175–176, 177; Getting around the Plane for, 118, 120, 121; Inside Pascal's Triangle for, 261, 263, 264, 265; Make a Fake for, 94, 97; Museum of the Very Large and Small for, 240, 243–244; Pattern Carnival for, 153, 154, 156, 157; Picking Paintings Apart for, 83, 84, 85–86; Pieces and Parts for, 180, 183, 184; Seeing Expressions for, 250, 252, 255; Seeing Growth on a Graph for, 159, 160, 161, 162, 163, 164; Ship Shape for, 124, 126, 127; Solids, Inside and Out for, 25, 28–29; Squares with a Difference for, 101, 102, 105, 106, 107; The Sum of the Parts for, 187, 189, 190–191; Table Patterns for, 133, 134–138; Two-Pattern Tango for, 145, 148; The Unit You for, 226, 229–230; Wondering with Fractions for, 67, 68, 70, 71

Dividing, 210

Division. *See* Fraction division

Dorsal visual pathway, 10–11

Dot-card number talk. *See* Visual number talks

Double Concentric: Scramble, 90, 91

Drawing Solids Sheet, 25, 26, 28, 29, 32

Driscoll, Mark, 8

E

Eames, Charles, 239, 242, 243

Eames, Ray, 239, 242, 243

Einstein, Albert, 13

Empty space, volume of, 44–49, 51

England, 8, 53, 247

Equivalence. *See* Fraction equivalence

Estimating with Fractions Investigate activity. *See* Wondering with Fractions

Estimating with Fractions Play activity. *See* Fraction Blizzard

Estimating with Fractions Visualize activity. *See* Making Snowflakes

Estimation: in Filling Small and Large activity, 233, 234, 236, 237, 238; life importance of, 53; in Make a Fake activity, 98; Number sense and, 54; photos, 67, 68, 69, 70. *See also* Fraction estimation

Exploration: in A Box of Boxes, 44, 45, 46–47, 48; in Creating Cards, 201, 203, 204, 205; in Filling Small and Large, 233, 236–237; in The 1492 Problem, 268, 270–271; of Fraction Division Conundrum, 217, 219, 220; in Fractions in a Pan, 172, 175, 176; in Getting around the Plane, 118, 120–121; in inside Pascal's Triangle, 248, 261, 263, 264; in Make a Fake, 94, 96; in Making Snowflakes, 55, 58, 59; in Museum of the Very Large and Small, 239, 243; in Pattern Carnival, 153, 156; in Picking Paintings Apart, 83, 85; in Seeing Expressions, 250, 254; in Seeing Growth on a Graph, 159, 160, 162–163; in Solids, Inside and Out, 25, 28; in Squares with a Difference, 101, 102, 105–106; in Two-Pattern Tango, 145, 147, 148; in The Unit You, 225, 228–229; in Wondering with Fractions, 67, 69, 70

Exponents, 242, 249, 268, 269, 271

Expressions. *See* The 1492 Problem; Inside Pascal's Triangle; Seeing Expressions

Extension: of Creating Cards, 202, 205; of Cuisenaire Trains, 210,

213; of Filling Small and Large, 234, 237; of The 1492 Problem, 268, 271–272; of Fraction Blizzard, 62, 65; of Museum of the Very Large and Small, 240, 244; of Pieces and Parts, 180, 183–184; of Seeing Expressions, 250, 255; of Ship Shape, 124, 125, 127, 132; of Solids, Inside and Out, 25, 27, 29; of Squares with a Difference, 103, 106; of The Sum of the Parts, 187, 191; in Table Patterns, 133, 134, 136; in Two-Pattern Tango, 145, 146, 147, 148, 149; of Wondering with Fractions, 68, 70–71

F

Factorial, 249, 268, 269, 271

Factors, 171, 181, 184

Field's medal, 5

Filling Small and Large: agenda for, 233–234; comprehension questions for, 238; discussion in, 234, 237; estimation in, 233, 234, 236, 237, 238; exploration in, 233, 236–237; launching, 233, 234, 236; video making in, 223–224, 234, 237; volume in, 234, 235, 236, 237

Finger perception, 11

"A First Grader's Guide to the Galaxy," 223

Flexibility. *See* Number and symbol flexibility

Flip and multiply, 199

"Fluency without Fear" (Boaler and Williams), 2

Forgery. *See* Make a Fake

Forms of notation, 269, 271, 272

Fostering Algebraic Thinking (Driscoll), 8

Four-Quadrant Transportation Graph, 118, 119, 120, 123

The 1492 Problem, 248; agenda for, 268; comprehension questions for, 272; discussion in,
268, 269, 271, 272; exploration in, 268, 270–271; factorial in, 249, 268, 269, 271; language of mathematics in, 272; launching, 268, 269, 270, 271; posters in, 269, 270–271; sheets for, 268, 270–271, 273–277; visual number talk in, 270

Fraction Blizzard: agenda for, 61–62; comprehension questions for, 65–66; discussion in, 54, 62, 64–65, 66; launching, 61, 64; Play agenda in, 61, 64; posters in, 61, 62, 63, 64–65; struggle in, 54, 65, 66

Fraction division, 199–200

Fraction Division Conundrum, 200; agenda for, 217; comprehension questions for, 221–222; discussion in, 217, 218, 219, 220–221; exploration of, 217, 219, 220; language of mathematics in, 221; launching, 217, 219; number sentences in, 219; posters in, 217, 220, 221; quotients in, 217, 218, 220, 221; visual proof in, 217, 218, 219, 221

Fraction division Investigate activity. *See* Fraction Division Conundrum

Fraction division Play activity. *See* Cuisenaire Trains

Fraction division Visualize activity. *See* Creating Cards

Fraction equivalence, 81–82; NAEP question about, 169, 170

Fraction equivalence Investigate activity. *See* Squares with a Difference

Fraction equivalence Play activity. *See* Make a Fake

Fraction equivalence Visualize activity. *See* Picking Paintings Apart

Fraction estimation, 53–54

Fraction estimation Investigate activity. *See* Wondering with Fractions

Fraction estimation Play activity. *See* Fraction Blizzard

Fraction estimation Visualize activity. *See* Making Snowflakes

Fraction multiplication, 169–171

Fraction multiplication Investigate activity. *See* The Sum of the Parts

Fraction multiplication Play activity. *See* Pieces and Parts

Fraction multiplication Visualize activity. *See* Fractions in a Pan

Fractions in a Pan: agenda for, 172–173; Brownie Pan Template for, 179; comprehension questions for, 177–178; discussion in, 172, 173, 174, 175–176, 177; exploration in, 172, 175, 176; launching, 172, 175; number sentences in, 178; sheets for, 172, 175; visual proofs in, 170–171, 172, 175, 176, 177

G

Games. *See* Battleship; How Close to 100; Ship Shape

Generalization, 143, 144, 149, 160–161; Cuisenaire Trains and, 202, 205, 206; Fraction Division Conundrum and, 200

Generalizing, 160

Geometric art, 83, 84, 85, 94

Getting Around the Plane, 116; agenda for, 118; comprehension questions for, 121–122; dimensions in, 118, 119, 120, 121–122; discussion in, 118, 120, 121; exploration in, 118, 120–121; launching, 118, 119, 120; posters in, 118, 120–121; sheets for, 118, 119, 120, 123

Graphs: of Four-Quadrant Transportation Graph, 118, 119, 120, 123; of Plus-Sign Table and Graph Sheet, 166; of Where Is the Rectangle?, 129

Group work, 17–18

Testing: by NAEP, 169, 170; by PISA, 4; timed, 2; Youcubed score improvements for, 3

Three-dimensional figures, 33, 34

Three-dimensional representations of solids, 23, 25, 28, 30

Thurston, William, 5

Tiling, with wholes and pieces, 169–171

Trapezoid, 19, 20, 21

2 × 2 Square sheet, 101, 104, 111

Two-Dimensional Representations: of a Solid, 27; of three-dimensional space, 38

Two-Pattern Tango: agenda for, 145; color coding in, 144, 145, 146, 147; comprehension questions for, 148–149; discussion in, 145, 148; exploration in, 145, 147, 148; launching, 145, 147; Pattern A sheet, 145, 147, 151; Pattern B sheet, 145, 147, 152; posters in, 147, 155; sheets for, 145, 147, 148, 150–152; teacher notes for, 146

U

Unit, 226

The Unit You: agenda for, 225–226; comprehension questions for, 230–231; discussion in, 226, 229–230; exploration in, 225, 228–229; launching, 225, 228; sheets for, 225, 229, 232; teacher notes for, 226–227

The Unit You Organizer, 225, 229, 232

United Kingdom, 53

US News & World Report, 2

V

Videos: of Coordinate Plane, 115; in Filling Small and Large activity, 223–224, 234, 237; of "Powers of 10," 239, 242, 243; of visual number talk, 252

View, 28

Views. *See* City of Cubes; Solids, Inside and Out

Visual number talks: in The 1492 Problem activity, 270; in Seeing Expressions activity, 248, 250, 251, 252, 254; student status differences and, 12, 13; on Youcubed, 248, 252

Visual proofs, 7, 8; in Fraction Division Conundrum, 217, 218, 219, 221; Fractions in a Pan, 170–171, 172, 175, 176, 177; The Sum of the Parts, 187, 188, 189. *See also* Paper Folding activity

Visual thinking, 11

Visual understanding, of fraction multiplication, 170–197

Visualization activities: brain science of, 10–11, 23; for Coordinate Plane, 116, 118–123; creativity and, 12; engagement and, 11; for fraction estimation, 54, 55–60; number representation and, 10, 11, 12, 23; student status differences and, 12, 13. *See also specific Visualization activities*

Volume: in A Box of Boxes, 24, 44, 45, 46, 47, 48, 49, 51; in City of Cubes, 33, 37; of empty space, 44–49, 51; in Filling Small and Large, 234, 235, 236, 237; of Packing Boxes, 51; in Solids, Inside and Out, 27

W

Week of inspirational mathematics (WIM), 4, 12

What We Don't Like list, 17

Where Is the Rectangle?, 129

Wholes, tiling pieces with, 169, 170–171

"Why Math Education in the U.S. Doesn't Add Up" (Boaler and Zoido), 4

Williams, Cathy, 1; "Fluency without Fear" by, 2

WIM. *See* Week of inspirational mathematics

Wondering with Fractions, 54; agenda for, 67–68; color coding in, 67, 70; comprehension questions for, 71–72; discussion in, 67, 68, 70, 71; exploration in, 67, 69, 70; launching, 67, 69; posters in, 67, 70; sheets for, 67, 69, 70, 71–72, 73–79; teacher notes for, 68

Worksheets. *See* Sheets

Y

Youcubed: conception of, 1; finger perception on, 11; "four 4s problem" on, 248–249; low-floor, high ceiling activities and, 2–3; Strogatz featured on, 247–248; summer camp of, 3–4, 5–6, 115; summer school and, 12; videos on, 115; visual number talks on, 248, 252

Z

Zoido, Pablo, 4